A HISTORY OF
AMERSHAM

Aerial view of Amersham, 1928.

A HISTORY OF
AMERSHAM

Julian Hunt

Phillimore

2001

Published by
PHILLIMORE & CO. LTD.
Shopwyke Manor Barn, Chichester, West Sussex

ISBN 1 86077 187 4

Printed and bound in Great Britain by
BIDDLES LTD.
Guildford, Surrey

Contents

List of Illustrations

Frontispiece: Amersham from the air in 1928

Acknowledgements

I would like to record my gratitude to Barney Tyrwhitt-Drake, who encouraged me to write this book. He contributed greatly to the chapter on the Drake family and kindly provided notes on Amersham International. I am extremely grateful to Colin Seabright of Chesham Bois for loaning so many of his postcards and letting me see the deeds to his own house. I received valuable help from Monica Mullins of Amersham Museum, and Dr. Michael Brooks shared his research on the old Grammar School building. Richard Ayres supplied the notes on the Hatch family. Gill Thompson showed me the minutes of the Amersham Public Utility Society. Clive Foxell gave me useful advice on the Metropolitan Railway. I was also able to discuss the early history of Amersham Common and Wycombe Heath with the late Arnold Baines.

The photographs are largely from the County Records and Local Studies Service, Buckinghamshire County Museum and Amersham Library. These were supplemented by over 30 postcards loaned by Colin Seabright: 5, 26, 29, 31, 39, 40, 46, 64, 65, 67, 72-3, 79, 80, 83, 88, 91, 96, 99, 101, 103, 108-9, 111, 114, 116-8, 120, 125-6, 134, 136-7. James Venn of Great Missenden loaned items 3, 9, 10, 30, 34, 36, 42-3, 77, 81, 106-7, 112-3, 115, 123. Several photographs are from the Royal Commission on the Historical Monuments of England: 19, 21, 25, 71, 74-5, 82, 124. Ray East of Chesham supplied photograph 53. Richard Ayres loaned illustration 56. Gill Thompson loaned items 130-1. My father, Joseph Hunt, found the architect's drawings in the Studio Yearbook of Decorative Art. Peter Hoare of Cublington copied several maps and old photographs with his usual skill and patience.

The High Street and Town Hall in 1928.

Foreword

Amersham today is a fascinating town for the historically curious that has long cried out for a readable yet scholarly history. I am pleased to say that this has now come to pass with Julian Hunt's latest work in the Phillimore series of town histories. The development of the town of Amersham over the past 400 years in particular has been closely tied to the Drake family of Shardeloes. Today there are only two family members of my generation who still live in the area, and my cousin Bill Tyrwhitt-Drake remains Lord of the Manor of Amersham, so the family connections have yet to finish.

Two years ago I led a short walking tour of Amersham for members of the Bucks Genealogical Society. It was clear to us then that Amersham packs a great deal of evidence of both local and national history into a small area. I hope this book will encourage you to go out and see it for yourself and possibly join the Amersham Society which holds regular meetings devoted to the history of the town.

Barney Tyrwhitt-Drake
Great Missenden, 2001

One

Amersham in Domesday Book

In trying to grasp the history of a Buckinghamshire town, it must be accepted that its origin will often pre-date any event for which there is documentary evidence. It must also be recognised that any field boundaries, street patterns and house structures seen today are unlikely to be the earliest that have existed on the site. The historian can be excused therefore in commencing a history in 1086, when an understanding of earlier periods depends largely on place-name evidence and random archaeological finds from a wider area. Towns like Amersham emerge from the obscurity of the Dark Ages into the glittering light of Domesday Book, populous, productive and full of economic potential.

In 1066, the sprawling Chiltern parish of Amersham was already divided into six estates. The largest of these units was part of a portfolio of Crown property in Buckinghamshire, including lands in Chesham, Eton, Marlow and High Wycombe, which Edward the Confessor had settled on his wife, Queen Edith. As William the Conqueror claimed to be the rightful heir of King Edward, he could hardly dispossess Edith, even though she was the sister of the defeated Harold, so ownership of her Buckinghamshire estates remained unchanged until she died in 1075. Her land then reverted to the Crown and her manor of Amersham was granted to Geoffrey de Mandeville, who already owned seven other estates in Buckinghamshire.

The Manor of Amersham

The precise wording of the Domesday entry for Amersham is as follows:

> Geoffrey de Mandeville holds Amersham. It answers for 7½ hides. Land for 16 ploughs; in lordship 2 hides; 3 ploughs there. 14 villagers with 4 smallholders have 9 ploughs; a further 4 possible.

> 7 slaves; meadow for 16 ploughs; woodland 400 pigs. The total value is and was £9; before 1066 £16. Queen Edith held this manor.[1]

In common with many royal estates, Queen Edith's manor of Amersham enjoyed a very low rate of taxation. Estates were taxed according to their agricultural potential, normally measured in 'hides', or areas of arable land extending to about 120 acres. A typical Buckinghamshire village in Domesday Book is valued at 10 hides and often has the same number of ploughs at work. Queen Edith's estate at Amersham was valued at 7½ hides, yet there were three ploughs on her home farm and nine more shared between 18 tenant farmers and smallholders. The presence of seven slaves may be explained by the practice of employing convicted prisoners on royal estates. Meadow land was highly valued, for, even in the warm climate of the 11th century, it was not easy to grow enough grass to over-winter the oxen which pulled the ploughs. In fact there was so much meadow on Geoffrey de Mandeville's estate that the assessors noted there was sufficient for four more ploughs. The estate also had ample woodland, which, although crudely measured as an area sufficient to support 400 pigs, would have provided a surplus of structural timber and firewood which could be sold outside the parish. It would be normal practice for the owner of an estate the size of Amersham to provide a corn mill, where the tenants would have to grind their corn. As there is no mention of a mill on Geoffrey de Mandeville's property, we must assume the tenants were accustomed to use one or other of the three mills which stood on the smaller Amersham estates which had been detached from the main manor before 1066.

1 This view from Rectory Wood gives some impression of what Amersham might have looked like at the time of Domesday – a village of about twenty farmsteads, with at least 1,200 acres of arable land, ample meadow and woodland and three water mills.

Other Domesday Manors

Well before the Norman conquest, five farmsteads had been detached from the main manor of Amersham, each of them assessed at half a hide. It may be that Edward the Confessor, his wife Edith, or their predecessors, had given these estates to particularly loyal followers. It would have been politically difficult for King William to dispossess these Englishmen whilst they enjoyed the protection of Queen Edith, but all but one had been replaced by Normans by 1086.

> In Amersham Roger holds ½ hide from the Bishop [of Bayeux]. Land for 1 plough; it is there with 3 smallholders. 1 mill at 4s; meadow for 1 plough. The value of this land is and always was 20s. Alwin, Queen Edith's man, held this land; he could sell.

Alwin also occupied Queen Edith's estates at Dinton and Linslade.

> In Amersham Aelmer holds ½ hide from the Count [of Mortain]. Land for 2 ploughs; they are there, with 1 villager and 1 smallholder. Meadow for 2 ploughs; woodland, 20 pigs. The value is and always was 20s. Siward, Aldeva's man, held this land; he could sell.

Siward is described elsewhere in Buckinghamshire Domesday as a man of Earl Harold.

> In Amersham Wulgeat holds ½ hide from Hugh [de Bolbec]. Land for 2 ploughs; they are there with 2 villagers and 3 smallholders. 1 mill at 5s; woodland, 20 pigs. The value is and always was 20s. He also held it before 1066; he could sell.

Wulgeat is highly unusual as an Englishman who held on to his land, albeit as a sub-tenant of the new Norman owner, Hugh de Bolbec. He would have enjoyed the protection of Queen Edith until 1075, but he may have had another guarantor, as he is mentioned elsewhere in Buckinghamshire Domesday as a man of Wulfwig, Bishop of Lincoln.

> In Amersham Thurstan [Mantle] holds ½ hide. Land for two ploughs; 1 there; another possible. 2 villagers with one smallholder. Meadow for 2 ploughs; woodland, 30 pigs. The value is and was 13s 4d; before 1066, 20s. Thorkell, King Edward's man, held this land; he could sell.

Thorkell's estate is estimated to have been worth 20s. per year, exactly the same valuation as the other four half-hide manors in Amersham.

> Jocelyn the Breton holds ½ hide in Amersham. Land for 1 plough; it is there with 5 smallholders. 1 mill at 4s; meadow for 1 plough. The value is and always was 20s. Aelfric, Godric the Sheriff's man, held this land; he could sell

Owner in 1066	Owner and (sub tenant)	Tenant Farmers in 1086	Small-holders	Agricultural labourers	Hides	Ploughs	Mills (Value)	Woodland (Pigs)
Queen Edith	Geoffrey de Mandeville	14	4	7	7 1/2	12		400
Alwin a man of Queen Edith	Bishop of Bayeux (Roger)		3		1/2	1	1 (4s.)	
Siward a man of Aldeva	Count of Mortain (Aelmer)	1	1		1/2	2		20
Wulgeat	Hugh de Bolbec (Wulgeat)	2	3		1/2	2	1 (5s.)	20
Thorkell a man of King Edward	Thurstan Mantle	2	1		1/2	1		30
Aelfric a man of Godric the Sheriff	Jocelyn the Breton		5		1/2	1	1 (4s.)	
Totals		19	17	7	10	19	3	470

Aelfric, like the other four Saxon tenants at Amersham, was a freeholder. He would pay a token rent to his overlord, in this case Godric, Sheriff of Buckinghamshire and Berkshire in 1066.

Amersham's Agricultural Resources in 1086
The entries for the six Amersham estates are listed in Domesday Book according to the rank of their Norman overlords. Their agricultural potential is apparent from the table.

The table shows that Amersham and its sub-manors had an agricultural labour force of at least 43 men in 1086, which suggests a total population of about 215. Between them, Amersham's farmers

2 Pipers Wood is typical of Amersham's remaining woodland. At Domesday, the woodland was measured as sufficient for about 500 pigs to feed on the nuts and underwood. Most of the trees would have been pollarded, so as to produce a regular supply of firewood without cutting down whole trees.

3 At the time of Domesday, Amersham had three corn mills, two valued at 4s. each and one at 5s. Town Mill is almost certainly on one of these Domesday sites.

had 19 ploughs. The plough shares themselves were not of great value, but as each was pulled by a team of eight oxen, this represents 152 draught animals. Such a large number of animals which could not be slaughtered as winter approached would be a great burden on the farmers. It is recorded, however, that they had meadow land for 24 ploughs, meaning they could cut and store sufficient grass to feed 192 oxen during the winter. Their meadow by the river was probably supplemented by permanent pasture on Amersham Common and Wycombe Heath, which these animals could graze

for at least part of the winter. The Domesday assessors certainly didn't see lack of pasture as a problem, for they noted that there was sufficient land for six more ploughs. Three of the smaller estates in Amersham had water mills, together worth 13 shillings, which would have produced more flour than the local bakers could have consumed. The area of woodland around Amersham was quantified as enough to support 470 pigs, but its real value was as a source of wood for building and for fuel.

It is tempting to link Amersham's five smaller Domesday estates with farms which appear on the

4   The village of Coleshill was anciently an upland pasture belonging to the Manor of Tring. Its association with Tring predates the formation of English counties and it is therefore listed in the Hertfordshire section of Domesday Book.

modern map. Three of them had water corn mills, confirming that some of their land was adjacent to the River Misbourne. Three of them had significant areas of woodland, but this may be explained by their proximity to Amersham Common or to Wycombe Heath, where the neighbouring farmers claimed unlimited grazing and the right to cut the wood growing there. Mantles Green Farm might have its origin in the half hide belonging to Thurstan Mantle in 1086. Weedon Hill Farm might also be associated with the Count of Mortain's half hide, because the tenant, Aelmer, also held the hamlet of Weedon in Hardwick, a vale parish just north of Aylesbury. Such simplistic connections should be resisted, however, for the arable land belonging to these five ancient units may well have been inter-mixed in the common fields of the parent manor. Further sub-manors, like Raans, Shardeloes and

Woodrow, were detached from the main manor of Amersham after the Conquest, further complicating the pattern of land ownership.

The Manor of Coleshill

The Domesday subdivision of Amersham was further complicated by the fact that the hamlet of Coleshill was reckoned as part of Hertfordshire. The Domesday Book entry for Tring includes a two hide 'berewick', or distant farmstead, where eight farmers had two ploughs.[2] That this entry refers to Coleshill is confirmed by a royal grant of 1151 in which Tring and its distant sub-settlement are given to the Abbey of Faversham in Kent. These possessions soon reverted to the Crown and Coleshill was granted in 1175 to the Mandevilles, lords of the manor of Amersham. Coleshill, however, remained in Hertfordshire and

5 The Bury Farm was the equivalent of Amersham's manor house and would anciently have been the home of the lord of the manor's agent.

this anomaly was only corrected by an Act of Parliament of 1844, whereby various detached parts of English counties were absorbed into the surrounding county.

Domesday Book therefore gives us a picture of a prosperous agricultural community in Amersham. With light taxes and the advantage of three watermills, Amersham farmers were in an excellent position to cultivate more wheat than they needed and to produce enough flour to sell in neighbouring markets. With ample woodland, and access to two very extensive wooded commons, they could also produce a surplus of timber and firewood. As they lived only 26 miles from London, it is entirely possible that they were marketing their surplus in the capital even in 1086.

Life on the Medieval Manor

Geoffrey de Mandeville, who was given Queen Edith's 7½-hide estate in Amersham in 1075, appears not to have had a tenant at Amersham, but to have run the estate through his own agent. His home farm, which we can confidently associate with the present-day Bury Farm, was assessed at two hides and there were three ploughs at work on it. The Bury Farm was the equivalent of a manor house and Geoffrey de Mandeville's agent would hold a court there at least twice a year, with every tenant required to attend or face a stiff fine. These tenants were called copyholders, because their leases would be copies of the court rolls of the year in which they first rented or inherited their land. The leases would not only record the money rents payable,

6   The Bury Mill was purchased by William Drake with the manor of Amersham in 1637. It remained part of the Drake estate until the great sale of 1928.

but would also stipulate the number of days each tenant farmer was required to plough the land and harvest the crops on the lord of the manor's own farm. If a copyholder died, his successor would have to pay a 'heriot', a sort of inheritance tax, to the lord of the manor, usually the best animal on the farm concerned. The copyholder even had to pay a fine if his son left the village, or his daughter wanted to get married. Copyhold tenants were also obliged to grind their corn at the manorial mill. Surprisingly, Domesday Book does not record a mill on Geoffrey de Mandeville's estate at Amersham, but the Bury Mill (still standing beside the present-day *Chequers Inn*), would soon be added to the facilities of the manor as a further means of extracting the maximum income from the tenants.

Two

A New Town in the Chilterns

The Borough of Amersham

It is estimated that the population of England at Domesday was about 1,500,000 and that this had doubled by the time the Black Death struck in 1348. This was a time of rapid economic as well as population growth, which saw the development of a mercantile class fitting in the social hierarchy somewhere between the lord of the manor and the tenant farmer. Farmers, who had managed to save some of their surplus and pass it on to their children,

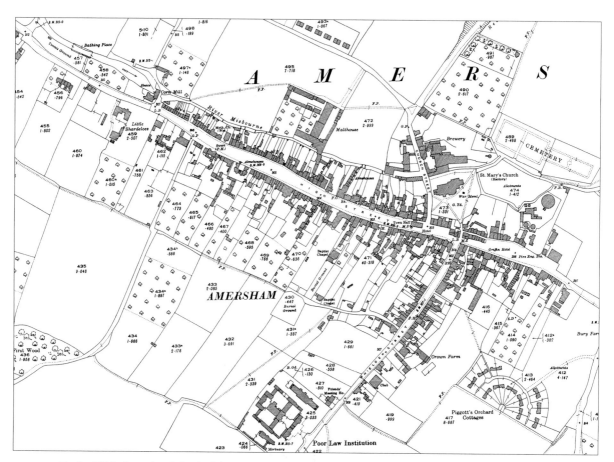

7 In 1200, Amersham's lord of the manor procured a royal charter to hold a Friday market and a September fair. Building plots for tradesmen's houses were set out on the south side of the London road, leaving ample space for market stalls. This map of 1923 shows how each plot could be accessed from a back lane, now called the Common Plat.

8 This view of the annual fair in the 1930s gives some idea of what Amersham's medieval fair might have looked like, with stalls occupying the length of the High Street and Broadway.

steered some of their younger sons into trade. The millers, corn merchants, blacksmiths, clothiers, dyers, fullers, tanners, saddlers, shoemakers, masons and carpenters, who turned many a medieval village into a town, might rent a workshop from the lord of the manor, but they had no time or inclination to plough the lord's fields or harvest his crops. They demanded, and usually got, a different kind of tenure from the lord of the manor, whose rent-roll would increase according to the number of tradesmen he could attract to his embryo town.

It became fashionable during the medieval period for proprietors of manors on good roads, or with other natural advantages, to earmark a part of the village as a market place and to charge tolls and stallage to those who wished to sell goods there. The Crown encouraged this trend and secured a healthy income by issuing royal charters, allowing an annual fair and or a weekly market. Nearby High Wycombe, sometimes styled Chepping Wycombe (the prefix meaning market), already had a market and needed no expensive licence to continue it. Geoffrey, Earl of Essex, nevertheless thought it worthwhile to obtain such a charter for Amersham in 1200, which permitted him to hold a Friday market and a fair on 7 and 8 September, being the day before and the day of the nativity of the Virgin Mary.[1] This date had more than religious significance, since it followed the harvest and preceded the slaughter of animals which were not to be over-wintered.

It is not clear when the Earl of Essex began to relax some of the conditions imposed on his agricultural tenants in order to attract tradesmen to live and work in Amersham. It was probably soon after he purchased the market charter in 1200 that he laid out 'burgage plots', that is uniform pieces of land, with street frontages of about twenty feet, stretching back about 200 feet to a rear access lane called the Common Plat. These plots were offered to 'burgesses', that is bakers, butchers, drapers, tailors and other useful tradesmen, at advantageously low rents, free of any duty to help out on the Bury Farm. There is no evidence that Amersham's burgesses were given control of the market place or allowed to set up trade guilds. They would, however, attempt to exclude from their market tradesmen from nearby towns and ensure that new entrants to their respective trades passed through a proper apprenticeship.

9   Amersham was principally a market for grain, but cattle and sheep were sold in the market place. Many of the bargains would be struck in the parlours of the inns and beerhouses in the High Street.

Burgage plots are clearly visible in old Amersham today, where the inns, shops and houses to the south and west of the High Street and Whielden Street all have back yards of equal dimensions, accessed from the Common Plat. Burgage tenure only extended to those properties belonging to the Earl of Essex, and an 18th-century map of the Borough of Amersham clearly shows that occupants of houses on the north side of the High Street, which belonged to the rector of Amersham, had no vote.[2] The borough was planned on a grand scale with a vast market area extending west from the church as far as the Town Mill. Not even High Wycombe can rival Amersham's High Street in length and width and the quality of the houses on its south side.

Amersham evidently developed very rapidly, for, by 1300, it was one of only 100 towns in England whose burgesses were invited to send representatives to Edward I's Parliament. This was a dubious privilege, since the King only summoned Parliament to broaden the base of consent to his unusually high taxation. There are records of five occasions in the reigns of Edward I and Edward II when representatives of Amersham attended Parliament, but the expense of travel and accommodation may have deterred the burgesses from sending two of their number to subsequent Parliaments. It was not until the 17th century that Amersham had residents of sufficient wealth and ambition to rejoin the political life of the nation, and reclaim the right to send two MPs to Parliament.

The Fraternity of St Katherine
In 1490, Drew Brudenell, of Chalfont St Peter, left 20 shillings in his will to the Fraternity of St Katherine in Amersham.[3] Such fraternities were set

10 Amersham's medieval planners laid out a market area extending nearly half a mile from the Broadway to the Town Mill.

11 Such was the width of the planned medieval market area, that stallholders whose families had traded there for generations were allowed to build cottages on the site of the former stalls and still leave room for the passage of traffic.

12 Turpin's Row took its name not from the highwayman, but from an 18th-century owner, Thomas Turpin. These houses were in the Borough of Amersham, and were bought by William Drake about 1790 to secure the tenants' votes.

13 The houses on the north side of the High Street, from Turpin's Row to the *Red Lion Inn*, were in the manor of Amersham rectory and their occupants had no votes in borough elections. The Drake family, therefore, bought less property on this side of the street.

14 John Leland described Amersham as 'a right pretty market [town] on Friday, of one street well built with timber'. His description might apply to the High Street even today, but his positive view of the commercial health of the town in the 16th century is particularly significant.

up by tradesmen in market towns to support members who had suffered illness or other loss of business. They often had charitable objectives such as the maintenance of the poor and the repair of roads and bridges. They sometimes appointed priests to say mass in the parish church for the souls of departed members. This was clearly the case in Amersham, where Thomas Nash, who died in 1521, left 2d. to the mother church of Lincoln, 3d. to the high altar of Amersham and 2d. to the altar of St Katherine. Because it had endowments to maintain a chapel and to pay a priest's salary, the Fraternity was regarded as a chantry and was therefore dissolved along with all other chantries during the reign of Edward VI. At this time the Fraternity was valued at £4 7s. 6d. and the priest's salary given as £3. The Fraternity building, which stood between the market place and the churchyard, passed to the churchwardens of Amersham and became known as the Church House. From 1624 it accommo-dated Dr. Challoner's Grammer School.[4] Two of the original 16th-century roof trusses, which no longer take the full weight of the roof, can still be seen behind the large 18th-century windows of the schoolrooms.

Amersham Market

John Leland, visiting Amersham about 1540, described it as 'a right pretty market [town] on Friday, of one street well built with timber'.[5] The market day was changed to Tuesday by a new charter obtained by Edward, Earl of Bedford, in 1613. The charter enabled the town to hold a fair on Whit Monday as well as the Autumn fair, which was set at 19 September. This latter fair, which followed the harvest, also became a statute fair, where live-in farm servants were hired for the forthcoming year. The lord of the manor benefited from the special tolls charged at such a fair, the farmers stood to sell more produce and cattle and the tradesmen, especially the publicans, could expect unusually brisk business. The fairs did, however, attract an unruly and sometimes lawless group, who travelled from fair to fair and introduced the element of the funfair into what was principally an agricultural event. It was this element which was to give fairs a bad name, especially in a town where long-established non-conformist congregations and their ministers took the lead in condemning the licentiousness so obvious on these occasions.

Three

Amersham Farms and Farmers

The Medieval Landscape

The typical midland settlement, typified by the 1500-acre parishes of north Buckinghamshire, had three large fields in which individual farmers had perhaps sixty half-acre strips of land scattered over the whole parish. When the community got together to sow wheat on one of the three fields, each farmer would therefore have about twenty acres of the crop. When they planted peas and beans on a second field, he would have a similar portion of the harvest. His cows and sheep would be pastured on the third field, their droppings ensuring that it was fertile enough to become the wheat field in the next season. His farmhouse would

15   When William Drake bought the manor of Amersham in 1637, the Bury Farm was tenanted by Sir Thomas Saunders, who paid a rent in kind of 84 quarters of malt.

be located next to those of other farmers around a village green or in a main street. It was once thought that this style of farming, and the settlement pattern which went with it, did not extend to the Chilterns, where parishes were much larger and where wide areas were given over to woodland and permanent pasture. According to a 1629 rental of William Drake of Shardeloes, however, his farms in the Chesham hamlet of Chartridge did have strips of arable land in common fields. Early deeds to farms in Coleshill show that this Amersham hamlet had at least three common fields, including the intriguingly named Church Field and Gospel Field.[1] Later deeds to the farms at Woodrow show that this hamlet too had a set of open fields including Pine, or Pint Pits Field, and Manly Field. If open-field farming was normal practice in neighbouring parishes and hamlets, it is inconceivable that the fashion for common arable farming was not followed in Amersham itself.

No deeds to the manor of Amersham have come to hand earlier than its sale in 1637 from the Earl of Bedford to William Drake of Shardeloes.[2] At this time, the 'capital messuage or manor house of Amersham … called the Bury' was leased to Thomas Saunders and Francis his brother for the unusual rent in kind of 84 quarters of malt per year. The estate included the Bury Mill, let to Tobias Saunders, Stockings Farm in Coleshill, let to Walter Tredway, and valuable tracts of woodland extending as far as Beaconsfield parish. The property was 'situate lying and being in the towns, fields, parishes and hamlets of Amersham and Beaconsfield'. In contemporary descriptions of settlements with strip farming, the term 'field' is invariably applied to the common arable of the community. A crude map of the manor of Amersham was produced to facilitate the 1637 sale.[3] It shows three large enclosures, south of the High Street, named Upper Bery Field, Lower Bery Field and Bery Field. The combined acreage of these

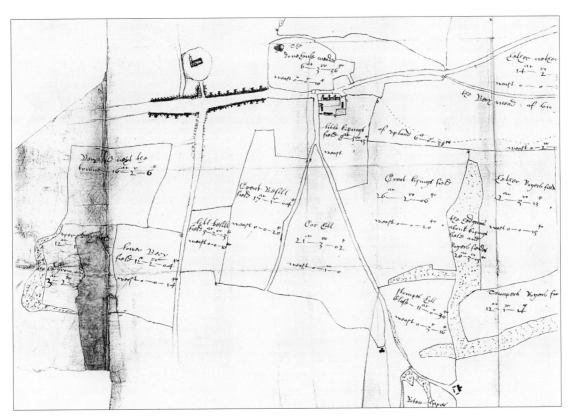

16 A map of the manor of Amersham, drawn up at the time of its sale from the Earl of Bedford to William Drake in 1637, gives the names of the large fields south of the town.

17   Crown Farm, Whielden Street, was bought by Thomas Tyrwhitt-Drake from William Child in 1813. It is one of the few farmhouses in the Borough of Amersham. It was subsequently called Crown Farm because the Drakes leased it to John Fowler, the tenant of the *Crown Inn*.

fields amounts to 52 acres, sufficient for the Bery Field to have been one of several open fields in which each sub-tenant in the town might have held several strips. South of the Bury Farm are Great and Little Besill Fields (23 acres), Great and Little Kipings Fields (35 acres) and Hither Rogers, Further Rogers and Trumpers Rogers Fields (49 acres). Between them is a triangular enclosure called Gor Hill (22 acres), 'gore' being the term for an awkward corner in a common field, where the strips are foreshortened. The layout of these fields suggests that a common-field system had broken down and that the process of enclosure was well advanced. There are several entries in Shardeloes estate rentals of the 17th century, where occupants of the larger houses on the High Street, such as the *White Hart Inn* (now called The

Worthies), rent ever smaller sub-divisions of the Bury Field. The success of Amersham as a market town may have made its inhabitants less dependant on their own farm produce and the lord of the manor more inclined to rent out the arable land in discreet blocks.

Amersham Common

Rivalling the growth of the new medieval town laid out by the River Misbourne was an unplanned but equally vigorous growth of farms and cottages around a clearing on the ridge between the Misbourne and Chess valleys. Quill Hall Farm, Raans Farm and Beel House are all ancient farmsteads, originally built on the perimeter of Amersham Common, but later approached by farm tracks

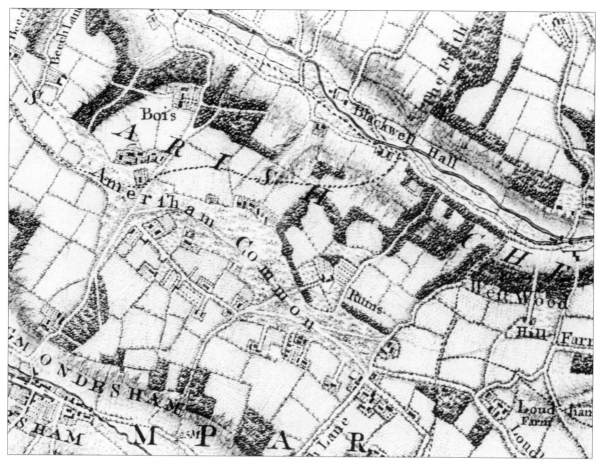

18 Rocque's map of Berkshire extends into south Buckinghamshire and includes the parish of Amersham. It is particularly useful in showing the farms around Amersham Common and the degree to which they had encroached onto the common by 1760.

through the new fields they had enclosed out of the common. Raans, though a grander building, is no more than an ancient farmstead, built on the edge of the common, with farmland developed by taking in some of the common in front of the house and clearing some of the woodland which sloped down to the River Chess at the rear.

When listed in early taxation returns or in estate rentals, the farms around Amersham Common are listed as part of a separate hamlet of Woodside. In order to distinguish one from another, these farms tended to assume the name either of the pioneer who established the farm, or, more likely, his successor who developed it further. Snells Farm, Cokes Farm, Bendrose Farm, Reeves Farm, and Hyrons Farm, all take their names from yeomen or tenant

farmers. Even a farm like Woodside Farm, sold by the executors of George Weller to the Metropolitan Railway Country Estates Ltd. in 1930, was earlier known as Pratt's Farm. Had this been clear to the Quaker historians who interpreted Mary Pennington's account of her sojourn at Woodside in 1668, they would have seen that she lived, not at Woodside Farm, now submerged in 'Metro-land', but at Beel House, which is often recorded as 'Pennington's' in the 18th century.[4]

Stanley Wood House was another old farmhouse once standing on the edge of Amersham Common, but later accessed by a private drive through the encroachments the owner had made on the common. On the chimney on the east wing was a datestone, IH 1678, probably referring to Jonas

19 Raans is an ancient farm whose enclosed arable fields and pastures were formed from clearing woodland to the north and encroaching on Amersham Common to the south.

20 Beel House was another prosperous farm, built up by exploiting the wood and pasture of Amersham Common. In the 1670s it was the home of the famous Quaker, Mary Pennington.

21 Reeves Farm was approached from White Lion Road via a private track, passing through the enclosures the tenant had taken out of Amersham Common. The farm was demolished in the 1950s to make way for a new school.

Harding of Woodside, an early supporter of the Baptist Meeting House in Amersham.[5] No doubt the house was once known as Hardings, but in the 19th century it became known as Moody's Farm, after the farmer who lived there in 1815 when Amersham Common was enclosed. By 1912, the house was no longer a farm and was given the name Stanley Wood House. It was demolished about 1960 and Little Reeves Avenue built on the site.

Alongside the large farmsteads on Amersham Common were a gaggle of cottages housing woodmen, turners, brickmakers, blacksmiths and beerhouse keepers, many of whom would have begun as squatters, keeping their houses by paying the modest fines the lord of the manor might impose for encroachments on the common.

At its largest extent, Amersham Common may have measured over 250 acres. Its survival depended on a balance between over-grazing, which would

22 All the farms and cottages around Amersham Common were entered in chief rentals and taxation returns as part of the hamlet of Amersham Woodside. They were distinguished merely by the name of their tenants, and, as late as 1839, Woodside Farm was known as Pratt's Farm.

have destroyed the trees, and growing too many trees for timber, which would have stopped the growth of underwood on which the animals could feed. The Common was traversed by the highway from Amersham to Rickmansworth which was later turnpiked as the Reading to Hatfield Road. A turnpike collector's house was built on this road

just north of Beel House. Old-established pubs on the Common, such as the *Black Horse* and the *White Lion*, served travellers on the turnpike road, but beerhouses like the *Boot and Slipper*, the *Red Lion*, the *Pheasant* and the *Pineapple*, first licensed in 1830 but evidently much older, served a local need. The fact that there are six old pubs around the Common

23 Woodside Farm was purchased in 1930 by Metropolitan Railway Country Estates Ltd. This extensive range of barns was used by a haulage firm until converted into a community centre in 1955.

24 The old stables at Woodside Farm were used by an upholstery firm, until adapted to accommodate adult education classes in 1955.

25 Stanley Wood House was another old farmhouse, once standing on the edge of Amersham Common but later hidden by the enclosures the owner had taken out of the common. The site of the house is now occupied by Little Reeves Avenue.

26 The *Pineapple Inn* is set back from White Lion Road because earlier occupiers of the land either side had moved their fences forward onto Amersham Common to extend their arable land.

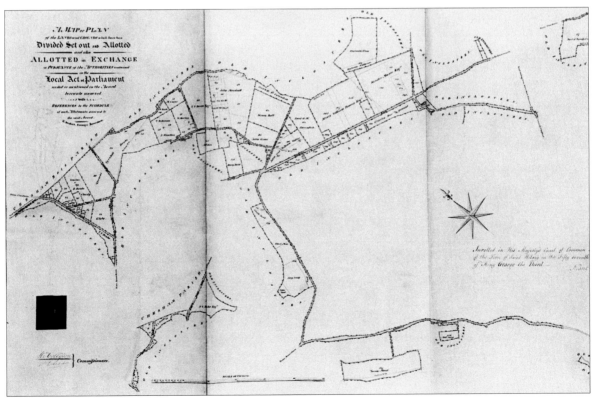

27 The remainder of Amersham Common was enclosed by Act of Parliament in 1815. This map is attached to the enclosure award.

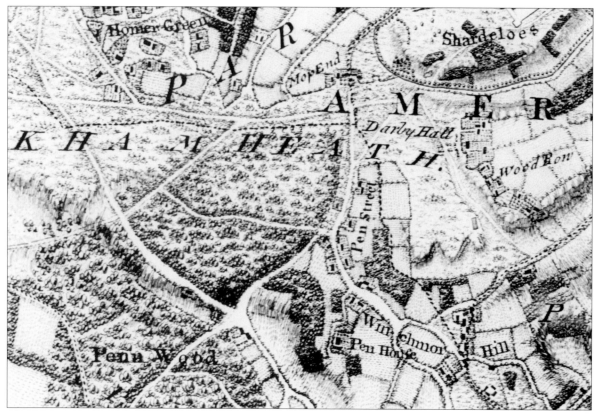

28 Rocque's map, drawn about 1760, shows the eastern end of Wycombe Heath extending to Woodrow and Winchmore Hill.

shows what a thriving sub-settlement existed on its perimeter.

Having withstood centuries of over-grazing and encroachment, Amersham Common was finally enclosed by Act of Parliament in 1815, along with all the other common land in the parish. The Act lists several landowners who were the key promoters of enclosure, including Thomas Tyrwhitt-Drake, lord of the manors of Amersham, Weedon Hill and Woodrow, the Rev. John Drake, rector of Amersham, George Henry Cavendish, lord of the reputed manor of Raans, and Kendar Mason, owner of Beel House and several farms on the south side of the Common. The Act appointed William Collison of Brackley and William Davis of Chenies as impartial commissioners, who would divide the land between all those who could prove a claim on the common. In the subsequent Enclosure Award,

the bulk of Amersham Common was allotted to Kendar Mason and his brother, William Henry Pomeroy. George Henry Cavendish was given two valuable allotments either side of Raans Road. Other significant allotments were to the Amersham solicitor John Marshall, owner of Quill Hall, and the brewers, John and William Weller, who had been buying land around the Common, probably in anticipation of enclosure. Thomas Tyrwhitt-Drake of Shardeloes accepted a relatively small part of Amersham Common, probably because the commissioners were also dividing Wycombe Heath, where he successfully claimed a large allotment near his own house.

Wycombe Heath

A similar community of independent-minded cattle farmers and woodmen had grown up around Wycombe Heath on the south-west boundary of

29 Woodrow High House was originally a farm whose real value lay in its right to pasture large numbers of cattle on Wycombe Heath.

Amersham. The Heath once extended over 4,000 acres and included much of the higher land of Penn, High Wycombe, Hughenden, Great Missenden, Little Missenden and Amersham. Part wood and part rough pasture, the Heath was grazed by cattle, sheep and pigs. Farmers on the edge of the Heath could build up profitable herds which their enclosed land could never have supported. An important farm such as Woodrow High House would have developed from such a cattle farm.

The Heath also provided a livelihood for woodmen, charcoal burners, potters and brickmakers. William Slade, who died in 1763, is one of the first potters to be identified in the parish registers. Three pothawkers, one corkman and one rabbit man are listed amongst the able bodied men of Woodrow hamlet in 1798.[6] As more and more cottages were built by industrious squatters on the edge of the Heath, hamlets emerged and grew into large

settlements like Holmer Green, Penn Street and Woodrow. The inhabitants of these hamlets, living and working at a distance from their village or town centres, were served by beerhouses such as the *Old Griffin* at Mop End, the *Queens Head* at Coleshill and the *Plough* and the *Potters Arms* at Winchmore Hill.

The obvious tension between the graziers and the woodmen of Wycombe Heath was resolved by the expedient of pollarding mature trees so that new growth to be used as firewood was beyond the reach of grazing animals. Any attempts by the lords of the manor of neighbouring parishes to enclose the Heath were met with implacable opposition by the commoners. They took their rights so seriously that they even resorted to forgery to back up their claims. Copies of a 'royal charter' of 1666, giving the bounds of the Heath and listing the privileges of those who lived on its perimeter, survive locally. The authors of this forgery displayed

30 Mop End was a hamlet on the edge of Wycombe Heath. The *Old Griffin Inn* would have been frequented by local farmers and woodmen.

31 The common at Winchmore Hill is a tiny remnant of Wycombe Heath. The *Potters Arms* can be seen to the right of an old pottery kiln.

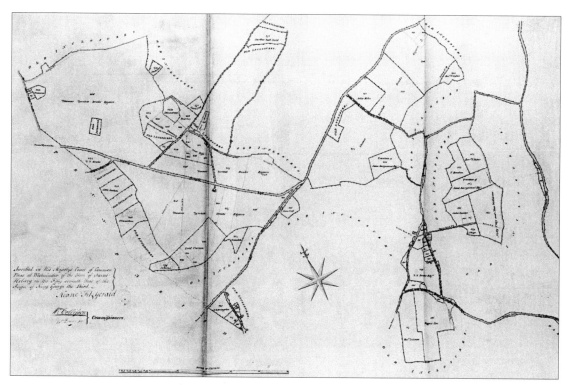

32 The portion of Wycombe Heath within the parish of Amersham was enclosed by Act of Parliament in 1815. This detail of the enclosure map shows how the land was divided amongst the neighbouring landowners.

a good knowledge of the landscape but a rather shaky grasp of legal phraseology.[7]

Wycombe Heath came under increasing pressure in the 18th century. Year after year, the Amersham court books list the encroachments made by neighbouring landowners and the fines imposed on the culprits. In 1733, the lord of the manor, William Drake, was himself accused of setting up the paling of his park on the waste at Wycombe Heath.[8] A substantial farmer like William Child of Woodrow was not averse to taking in some of the common land. In 1771 he was fined 10s. for a one-acre encroachment near his own house. The boundaries of the various parishes surrounding the Heath were not apparent on the ground, so it is not surprising that several of the encroachments mentioned in the Amersham court books were made by residents of Penn Street pushing their enclosed land north-eastwards over the invisible line into Amersham parish. Wycombe Heath, like Amersham Common,

was crossed by the main road from Amersham to High Wycombe. When this road was turnpiked in 1768, the value of neighbouring land increased and gave further incentive to the locals to take in plots of land adjacent to the road. A turnpike collector's house was erected on Whielden Lane, on the boundary of the Heath within Amersham parish.

The Act of Parliament under which Amersham Common was enclosed in 1815 also brought about the division of that part of Wycombe Heath which lay within Amersham parish. Apart from a modest allotment to Thomas Windsor of Woodrow High House, the bulk of the land was given to Thomas Tyrwhitt-Drake as lord of the manor of Woodrow. The part of the Heath between Mop End and Woodrow was fenced off as an extension to Shardeloes Park. Only that part between Woodrow and Penn Street was allotted to local farmers and given over to arable cultivation.

Four

Trade and Industry

Corn Mills

Like High Wycombe and Chesham, Amersham was principally a market for grain. If the town earned a reputation for supplying good quality wheat and barley, merchants would be content to buy a large consignment on inspecting a sample of the product on market day. Although the bulk of Amersham's grain production must have found its way to London, the town had its own corn mills, three of which are listed in Domesday Book. One of these must have been the Upper Mill, which belonged to the Cheyne family of Chesham Bois. In 1698, it was let for 99 years to John Charsley of Amersham, carpenter, at a rent of £28 per year.[1] John Charsley was evidently a very successful carpenter and applied his skill in

33   The Town Mill was an ancient corn mill, powered by a 9ft. diameter overshot water-wheel. It was used for the manufacture of paper in the late 18th century. It is sometimes called Sibley's Mill, after William Sibley and his son Albert, who were the last millers.

26

34 The Bury Mill was always a corn mill, and operated until its by-wash was affected by the building of Station Road in the 1890s. It was converted into the Mill Stream Café in 1934, when a dance floor and galleries were installed.

35 Liscar, or Hinton House, was the home of Robert Eeles, who held the lease of the Bury Mill in the late 18th century. The Eeles family were strong supporters of the Friends Meeting House.

36   Quarrenden Mill was a new corn mill built by William Holding on land leased from William Drake in 1766.

constructing water wheels and installing millstones to good effect. When Rebecca Charsley insured the mill with the Sun Fire Office in 1722, she valued it at £120, her house at £200 and its contents at a further £100. Charsley's Mill was purchased by William Drake in 1792. It was later known as Town Mill, or Sibley's Mill, after a 19th-century miller.

The Lower Mill, or Bury Mill, was also a profitable business. For much of the 18th century it was leased from the Drake family by Robert Eeles, a Quaker, who lived at what is now called Hinton House. The tenancy of a mill and the skills of a millwright were jealously guarded and handed down from father to son. Millers' sons also tended to marry millers' daughters. In 1759, Robert Eeles married the daughter of John Coles of Henley on Thames, also a mealman and also a Quaker. An inventory of the equipment at the Bury Mill was made in 1778, showing that, even at that date, the mill stones were of French origin.[2] The mill was

producing 54 sacks of flour per week in 1798.[3] Robert Eeles died in 1805 and was buried at the Friends Meeting House.

In 1766, William Drake leased a plot of land near Quarrenden Farm to William Holding of Amersham, mealman, on which an entirely new corn mill was built. Quarrenden Mill was later run by Joseph Impey, who was producing 48 sacks of flour per week in 1798. In 1851, John Impey, miller, employed one man at the mill, but he himself lived on the High Street, just to the east of Tothill's Workhouse. He also acted as the manager of the Friends Meeting House. He was running the mill in 1855 when it was burnt down. It was obviously repaired for it was advertised to be let at £60 per year in 1883. It was said to have an overshot water wheel and three pairs of stones.

Although windmills were a traditional feature of the Buckinghamshire landscape, they were less common in the Chilterns where water power was readily available. The windmill at Coleshill was

37 Coleshill Windmill was built by Thomas Grove in 1856. It was last operated by Alfred Pusey in 1903.

doubly unusual as it was erected as late as 1856, when steam power was beginning to supplement the power of windmill sails and water-wheels. It was built in the style of a Kentish windmill by Holmans of Canterbury. The owner was Thomas Grove. The mill was leased to a succession of millers and was last used by Alfred Pusey in 1903.

Maltings

If there is one feature which sets Amersham apart from other Buckinghamshire market towns it is the number of its maltsters and the early emergence of common brewers. Most towns had one or two maltings, supplying malt to local publicans who brewed beer on their own premises. There were few breweries outside London before the late 18th century, so the presence of an ancient brewery in Amersham says a lot about the importance of the town and the enterprise of its inhabitants. There is

a persistent local tradition that monks brewed beer in Amersham in the 15th century. The story may have arisen because Amersham's brewery stood by the church, whose revenues were given by the Earl of Essex to Walden Abbey as early as 1140. An alternative source of the tradition may have been a reference to Missenden Abbey in the deeds to one of the properties which were given to the Abbey by pious Amersham residents prior to the Reformation.

When William Tothill was negotiating to buy the Manor of Amersham from the Earl of Bedford in 1624, the rent of the Bury Farm, then leased to the prominent Saunders family, was 80 quarters of malt per year. At this time malt was sold for about £1 per quarter. Edward Perrott of Amersham, a wealthy Quaker, owned a malting near the church, which was later absorbed into Weller's Brewery. When Perrott died in 1665, his executors listed the

38   The building called Ye Olde Malte Tea House was an ancient malting belonging to the Wingfield family. It was purchased by William Weller in 1783 and run as part of Amersham Brewery.

following outstanding accounts for malt, which he had supplied to London brewers.[4]

	£	s.	d.
William Collens	68	16	0
William Collens for malt	19	1	2
John Collens of St Gyles for malt	36	6	6
William Bardon	5	0	0
John Bartholomew of Soohooe for malt	40	0	0
Joseph Lawrence of Old Street	150	0	0

Most of the larger inns in Amersham had their own maltings. Walter Webb was a farmer and maltster as well as an innkeeper. He owned the *Swan Inn* and also held a lease on the *White Hart Inn* (now known as The Worthies), both of which appear to have had maltings at the rear. When he died in 1675, he had barley growing in the field and more in the barn, together worth £23. He also had 'malt ready made' valued at £100.

The high value of maltings and malt is also apparent from early Sun Fire Insurance policies. In 1725, Hannah Grimsdale, widow, of Cokes Farm, insured a house near the *Crown Inn* occupied by William Hailey, and a malting and other buildings adjoining, for £300.[5] One of her tenants, John Brandon of Amersham, maltster, subsequently insured 'his goods and merchandise enclosed in his malting office and kiln and other outhouses, all adjoining, situate in the yard of William Hailey,' for a further £300. This house is now the post office.

The Hunt family had been maltsters in Amersham from the beginning of the 17th century and owned a house on the north side of the High Street, now the home of Amersham Museum.[6] In 1779, James Hunt of Amersham, maltster, insured his 'dwellinghouse, malthouse, granary and loft' for £280. He also insured the utensils and stock for £100. James Hunt died in 1783, but the malting was continued by his son-in-law, Daniel Bateman, into the 1800s. Another old malting stood behind the house now called Whyte Posts, on the south

39 The white house beyond the lamp post was the home of a wealthy maltster named Thomas Crouch who died in 1702. In recent years the house has become known as Whyte Posts.

40 The house on the left-hand side of the High Street, now occupied by Amersham Museum, was the home of another maltster, James Hunt, who died in 1783. His family were established as maltsters in the town at least as early as 1613.

41 Part of the new maltings, built for Weller's Brewery in 1829.

side of the High Street. This was purchased in 1632 by John Martlew, maltster, and sold in 1669 to Thomas Crouch, maltster, who ran the business until his death in 1702.[7]

The oldest surviving malting is the building on the north side of Broadway, recently known as the Ye Olde Malt Tea House. It was built in the 16th or 17th century and was owned by Nathaniel Wingfield from the 1720s. Wingfield's tenant, John Collingwood, also kept the *Griffin Inn* on the other side of the road. When William Weller purchased the malting from Wingfield's executors in 1783, it was known as the Griffin Malthouse. The largest malting premises are of course the new maltings built by Edward and William Weller in 1829, which are now home to a variety of small businesses.

The Brewery

The earliest known brewer in Amersham is Giles Watkins, who was born in Amersham in 1579. His sister Elizabeth married William Child of Amersham,

yeoman, in 1599, and his son, another Giles Watkins, was baptised at St Mary's in 1600. If we are to believe the re-cut date on the arch supporting that part of the brewery which stands over the River Misbourne, Watkins would have been building on this site in 1634. He was certainly one of the wealthiest men in Amersham in 1626, when he was assessed at £4 10s. 8d. for the lay subsidy.

Giles Watkins of Amersham, brewer, died in 1636. His executors, his son John and his brother-in-law William Child of Amersham, yeoman, had to dispose of an heirloom, described in his will as the 'drawing table over the brewhouse which was Robert Juckes'. John Watkins may well have taken his uncle into partnership. In 1637, William Child, brewer, gave a mortgage on a large house on the south of the High Street, whose outhouses included malthouses, maltlofts, barns, stables and granaries.[8] Mary, wife of John Watkins, brewer, was buried at St Mary's in 1639 and Giles, son of John Watkins, was buried there in 1643. John Watkins himself

42 Weller's Brewery was at one time the largest employer in Amersham.

43 Weller's Brewery closed in 1929, following its sale at auction to Benskins of Watford. The new owners were only interested in selling their own beers from the 133 tied houses.

may have died during the interregnum, when the parish registers were not properly kept. The brewery was probably carried on by the Child family, who also owned the *Crown Inn* and other valuable property in the town.

In 1679, William Ball of Amersham, brewer, leased three fields near Cherry Lane from William Drake. At this time, other members of the Ball family held the lease of the Bury Farm and William Ball's sister had married James Child. William Ball had other partners or tenants at the brewery, for John Perrott of Amersham, brewer, is mentioned in the Quarter Sessions records in 1693 and Richard Whitlock, gentleman, paid tax for the brewhouse in 1695. The brewery must have supplied most of Amersham's inns. William Ball himself owned the *Swan Inn*, his brother in-law James Child owned the *Crown*, and John Perrott leased the *White Hart* from William Drake. Richard Whitlock owned the *Red Lion*, which stood to the east of the *Crown* and ceased to be an inn about 1720. Richard Whitlock is cast as the villain in a letter of 1698, written by the curate of Amersham to Thomas Smith of Beaconsfield, the Drake family solicitor. The curate informs him that Mr. Whitlock, who was owed £6 rent by John Dummerton, of the *Red Lion Inn*, had seized all Dummerton's goods and left his wife and six children to starve in an empty house, 'to get possession of the house, to gain a vote'. Smith arranged for the debt to be paid and the receipt for £6, plus £8 costs, is dated 14 April 1699.[9]

William Ball had certainly given up running the brewery before his death in 1700. In his will he left to his wife Mary a 'messuage or tenement and brewhouse with the appurtenances wherein Richard Tipping now dwelleth situate and being in Amersham in the said County of Bucks and the use and occupation of the copper brewing vessels and utensils of or belonging to the said brewhouse'. He also left her the house next to the brewery (later known as Rumsey's), with 11 acres of land near Back Lane, including the Barn Close and Watkins Pightle.

The brewery continued to be operated by Richard Tipping, who was described as a 'common brewer' when accused at the Quarter Sessions in 1701 of supplying beer to an unlicensed beerseller, Isaac Carter. When Richard Tipping died in 1728,

the lease of the brewery was taken over by John Lawrence. Lawrence is variously described in contemporary documents as a brewer, or as a gentlemen. The brewery owner, Mary Ball, died in 1730 and, under the terms of William Ball's will, the brewery descended to his niece, Elizabeth Simpson. She was the daughter of William Simpson of Dunton, in north Buckinghamshire. A potential inheritance as valuable as Amersham's brewery had enabled her to marry Alexander Wallace, a wealthy London linen draper. The subsequent descent of the brewery is well documented in the court rolls of Amersham rectory. At the court of 1761, it was reported that 'Alexander Wallace, who held freely … one messuage or tenement wherein Mr. Lawrence now dwells … is dead … Elizabeth wife of George Mackrell is his only daughter'.[10]

Weller & Co.

John Lawrence of Amersham, brewer, died in 1764. In 1775, his son John Lawrence sold his interest in the brewery, along with the *Saracens Head* in Whielden Street and the *Old Griffin* at Mop End, to a High Wycombe maltster named William Weller. Weller insured the brewery with the Sun Fire Office in 1777. The contents of the brewery and the malthouse were valued at £200 each. The policy also covered the contents of a malthouse at High Wycombe valued at £400.[11] In 1783, William Weller bought the old malthouse on the north side of the Broadway from the executors of Nathaniel Wingfield. When William Weller died in 1802, the brewery was continued by his sons John Weller (1759-1843) and William Weller (1764-1843).

John and William Weller steadily increased the number of licensed premises belonging to the brewery. In 1802, they bought the *Chequers* at Bury End, the *Queens Head* in Whielden Street and the *Red Lion* at Coleshill. They bought two properties opposite the brewery in 1810 and 1812, where they built new cartsheds and stables. The Wellers' landlord, George Mackrell, had died in 1781, leaving the brewery to his wife Elizabeth. When she died in 1793, their daughter Elizabeth Ann Cooper inherited. She eventually sold the freehold to John and William Weller in 1818. Purchases of tied premises after this date covered a much wider area, with pubs as far away as

44 The Weller family once occupied a position in Amersham society second only to the Drakes of Shardeloes. John Weller lived at The Firs, now known as Piers Place, until his death in 1843.

45 Rumsey's, Church Street, once the home of Dr. James Rumsey, was purchased by William Weller in 1859.

Aylesbury and Harefield added to the chain. In 1829, John and William Weller built brand new malthouses in the meadows over the river from the High Street. It was here that a great fire in 1837 led to the destruction of about 1,500 quarters of malt and a loss to Weller & Co. of £5,000. Despite this setback, the brothers opened yet more pubs in Amersham: the *Red Lion*, High Street, in 1837; the *Eagle*, High Street, in 1838 and the *Wheatsheaf*, London Road, in 1842. John Weller lived in some style at The Firs, High Street, now known as Piers Place. His brother William rented the house east of the *Crown Inn*, which may still have had a malting at the rear. Both John and William Weller died in 1843, when the brewery was taken over by John's son Edward (1791-1850) and William's son William (1797-1859).

Edward and William Weller continued to add to the chain of tied premises with the purchase of the *Red Lion* at Amersham Common in 1848 and the *Boot and Slipper*, also on the Common, in 1849. Edward Weller lived at Swiss Villa, Turnham Green, Middlesex. He died there in August 1850, leaving the brewery in the sole ownership of William Weller. He was by now living at the house immediately north of the brewery, but in April 1859, he bought the neighbouring house which had belonged to James Rumsey, one of Amersham's most respected doctors. William Weller died in September 1859, but his widow, Lydia, lived at Rumsey's until her death in 1891.

The brewery passed to William Weller's three sons, William, Edward and George. William Weller remained a partner until his death at Springfield House, Hughenden, in 1908. Edward Weller lived for some years at the White House, in Church Street. In 1872, he married the daughter of the vicar of Chesham and moved to Blackwell Hall in Waterside, Chesham. He died at Brighton in 1890. It was George Weller (1844-1929) who became the managing partner in the brewery. He lived at The Plantation, Amersham Common, which he bought from Lord Chesham in 1885. He made several extensions and improvements to the house and, when a new school was built at Amersham Common in 1901, he turned the old schoolhouse on Raans Road into a lodge. The Wellers had purchased other agricultural land at Amersham

Common, including Woodside Farm. Part of this farm was sold to the Metropolitan Railway in 1887 for the construction of their extension to Aylesbury. The remainder was sold in 1930 to the Metropolitan Railway Country Estates Ltd. George Weller was quick to exploit the opening of the railway in 1892 by building the *Station Hotel* across the road from the station forecourt. This entailed the closure of an old beerhouse on Amersham Common called the *Black Horse* and the transfer of its licence to the new hotel in 1893.

In 1900, George Weller made his son, Gerrard Masterman Heath Weller (1873-1947), a junior partner in the brewery. The arrangement did not work out and, on the death of William Weller in 1908, George Weller bought up all the shares and continued the business on his own, with his son as manager and brewer. Gerrard Weller, who lived at Rumsey's, had decided not to continue the business even before his father died in 1929. The brewery was accordingly put up for auction in September 1929, when Benskins of Watford were the highest bidders, securing the brewery and 133 tied houses for £360,000. Production was moved from Amersham and the brewery premises sold to J.M. Long. In October 1929, George Weller died, aged 84. The Plantation was sold and eventually demolished for redevelopment in 1976.

Tanning

One of the definitions of a market town is the possession of a cattle market. Amersham's weekly market served the needs not only of its butchers, but also of its tanners and curriers, who processed animal skins for the town's shoemakers, glovers, breaches makers, saddlers and harness makers. Tanning required the use of large quantities of water for cleansing, processing and finishing the skins, so it is not surprising to find that the two principal tanning firms were situated on the north side of the High Street, with yards extending back to the River Misbourne. The earliest reference to a tannery in the town is in the will of Henry Bradshaw, of Amersham, tanner in 1569. The parish registers mention John Nash, tanner, in 1637, John Lered, tanner, in 1638, Abraham Greenaway, fellmonger, in 1662 and Thomas Jackson, currier, in 1679.

46 Amersham's largest tannery, run by the Salter family, was located behind the cottages on the extreme right of this photograph. The site was later used for the gas works, commenced in 1855.

47 On the south side of the Broadway was the entrance to a large house and a row of cottages occupied by Richard Norwood, a currier, or leather dresser, and his workmen.

48 Norwood's Yard took its name from Richard Norwood, whose family were in business here as curriers from the 1740s.

David Salter, of Amersham, tanner, appears in the Quarter Sessions records in 1693. Tanners ground up the bark of oak trees to produce tannin. Animal skins were repeatedly immersed in vats of tannin of varying strengths during processing. The offensive smell would have been a problem for neighbouring businesses and households.

Perhaps for this reason, David Salter occupied the last house on the north-east side of the Broadway, with his tanyard situated between the house and the River Misbourne. It was not a large house, but tax was paid in 1765 for 16 windows. Most of the premises were in the Borough of Amersham, but the Salters paid a chief rent to Amersham rectory for a small piece of land on which a bark kiln stood. There is a very full description of the tanyard in a Sun Insurance policy of 1781, when John Salter of Amersham, tanner and farmer, insured his dwellinghouse, brewhouse and bark barn, all under one roof, for £250. There were also two stables, two more bark barns, two drying

sheds and a leather house. John Salter was also a maltster, for he had another barn with £200 worth of barley and a kilnhouse with utensils and stock valued at £50. In all, John Salter's property was valued at £1,100. John Salter died in 1795. The tanyard was later sold by his grandson, Dr. John Brickwell, to William Morten. Morten's daughter Mary married a tanner from Chesham, John Garrett, who continued the business until about 1850, when both the Amersham and Chesham tanneries closed down.

Opposite Salter's tanyard on Broadway was a group of houses now known as Norwood's Court. In 1777, Richard Norwood of Amersham, currier and leather cutter, insured his house there for £300. It is unlikely that he could have undertaken many of the processes involved in the production of leather on the south side of the street where there was a very limited water supply. A further insurance policy of 1779 shows that Norwood in fact rented a bark barn, leather house and drying house in 'Wingfield's

49 Another old tannery, owned by the Wingfield family, was accessed through the gates of an ancient house on the High Street which later became a butcher's shop and belonged to J.R. Buckingham in the 1930s.

50 The Norwood family also ran an old established tannery near to the *Elephant and Castle*. The premises were approached through the entry on the extreme left of this photograph.

51 A cotton mill was built in 1789 to provide employment for the poor. The site was on the north side of the London Road, where the tall cottages can be seen beside the road. The building on the right is Brazil's sausage factory, built in 1929 on a site now occupied by Tesco's supermarket.

Yard' (between 39 High Street and the river) and another bark barn, drying shed and leather house at 'Mr Harding's Yard' (between 99 High Street and the river).

The tanyard at 39 High Street had belonged to Nathaniel Wingfield. At the division of his property in 1763, it was described as a 'tan yard with tan vats, grinding houses, barns, stables, yards, gardens and appurtenances, in the occupation of William Harding' and was valued at £64.[12] The premises were later used as a butcher's shop, run successively by James Rogers, Joseph Keen and John Gurney.

William Harding owned another tanyard at 99 High Street. This property is described in a deed of 1656, when Paul Lyne of Amersham, tanner, purchased a house 'within the fee or rectory of

Amersham' with barns, stables, yards, tanyards, tan vats, sheds, orchards and gardens.[13] This tanyard was later occupied by John Nash of Amersham, tanner, whose children were baptised at the parish church in 1700 and 1704. In 1720, Sarah Charsley insured her house, two tenements, the tanyard and other outhouses in the tenure of John Wright, Elizabeth Ratie and Ruth Nash for £300. By 1761, the tannery had been purchased by William Harding, tanner, who was buried at the Baptist Meeting House in 1776. His widow Sarah left them in her will of 1788 to James Norwood, brother of Richard Norwood, tanner. The premises were eventually bought by John and William Weller and connected to their new maltings, built over the river in Barn Meadow in 1829.

Woollen Cloth Manufacture

In common with most English market towns, Amersham had a small clothing industry. Many women would have the skill to spin yarn on a spinning wheel and there would be several handloom weavers in the town. The early parish registers rarely list occupations, but between 1638 and 1641 we find four weavers, William Rutt, Thomas Fisher, Richard Grey and Edward Perrott. In 1668, Elizabeth Rutt issued her own trade token, depicting a shuttle. The finishing of cloth required greater skill. As early as 1560, Robert Watford of Amersham, fuller, left a will. He would probably have shared the premises of a corn miller, using the power of the water-wheel to lift the fulling hammers which compressed and matted the fibres in loosely-woven cloth. If he had no successor in the town, Amersham clothiers could have taken their cloth to Bois Mill, a fulling mill on the River Chess. In 1637, Robert Burrow, shearman, appears in the registers and another shearman, William Child, is listed in 1642. They had the highly skilled task of cutting off any stray fibres left proud of the cloth's surface. Andrew Burrows issued a token bearing the clothmaker's arms in 1665. Dyeing the cloth was the job of Job Rayment, whose dyehouse behind the *Swan Inn* was purchased by William Drake in 1668. Perhaps the last clothworker in the town was Samuel Wyer, who lived in Whielden Street and left a will in 1710.

The Cotton Mill

When William Tothill's workhouse in the High Street closed in 1789, the Baptist minister, Rev. Richard Morris, put forward an alternative plan to employ the poor of the parish. He had grown up in Lancashire and had seen the huge growth of the cotton industry there. In partnership with a local plumber and glazier, Thomas Hailey, he designed and built his own cotton mill on a site just west of Bury Mill.[14] The mill employed 28 men, who spun yarn, probably on spinning jennies, and wove cloth on handlooms. A directory of 1792 enthused over 'a manufactory for cotton, by Messrs Morris, Hailey and Hailey, of all kinds of white cotton goods, by machinery of the newest, and some of it of peculiar construction'. In 1798, 33 Amersham men are named in the *Posse Comitatus* (a 1798 list of able-bodied

52 Amersham's lace merchants specialised in the supply of black lace. This lacemaker was photographed at Coleshill in 1910.

men who might serve in the army) as spinners or weavers, making the factory the biggest employer in the town. As was the case in Lancashire, the supply of cotton and the export of cloth was badly affected by the Napoleonic wars. The factory closed in 1809, but William Jennings, a London crape manufacturer, bought part of it for his silk-crape business. The factory is marked on the 1839 Tithe Map, but it may have closed down by 1851 when only four silk weavers are listed on the census.

Lace

The manufacture of bone lace was established in Bedfordshire and Buckinghamshire during the 16th century. Some have ascribed its introduction to Catherine of Aragon, who is said to have taught the craft to the women of Ampthill, where she was resident in 1531. Others have suggested that Protestant refugees from France and Holland brought the skill to this country later in the century. The first evidence of its importance to the local economy comes in 1592, when the overseers of Eaton Socon, in Bedfordshire, employed a woman to teach bone

53 The manufacture of straw-plait for the Luton hat industry provided employment when lace-making declined. The photographs shows an Amersham straw-plaiter with her plait mill.

54 The manufacture of chairs required little investment, either in premises or machinery. Here a local chair maker turns a chair leg on a pole lathe.

55 Joseph Hatch's chair factory at Whielden Gate, Amersham, 1910.

lace to the poor children of the parish. The term 'bone lace' was used either because the bobbins used to keep each thread under tension were made of bone, or because the threads were wound around bone needles pushed through holes in a leather pattern. The local drapers who supplied the linen thread and patterns to their cottage workers became known as lace buyers. The earliest evidence of an Amersham lace buyer is the token of William Statham of Amersham, issued in 1653. William Statham of Amersham, lace-buyer, is mentioned in the will of William Day, of Amersham, innholder, made in 1665. Daniel Anderson of Amersham, lace buyer, was party to a deed in 1690; Henry Hopper, laceman, insured his house in Amersham for £200 in 1721; William Statham of Amersham, laceman, was party to a deed regarding William Tothill's charity in 1723 and Giles Child, laceman, was buried at Amersham in 1757.

The lace buyers attended the Monday lace market at the *Bull and Mouth* in St Martin's by Aldersgate, or the Tuesday market at the *George Inn*, Aldersgate Street. Ann Morten of Amersham, 'dealer in lace', evidently kept part of her stock in a London inn for, in 1777, she insured her 'stock and goods in trust or on commission in her chamber in the *George Inn* on Snow Hill, for £200'.[15] In listing the chief manufactures of the town, the *Universal British Directory*, published in 1792, includes 'lace, which is considerably large, chiefly black lace'. The directory lists only one lace merchant, William Morten, who rented the house in the High Street originally bequeathed by William Tothill, in 1626, as a residence for the governor of the workhouse. There is no evidence, however, that William Morten used workhouse inmates to make lace. In 1823, the compiler of *Pigot's Directory* observed that 'the women and children are principally employed in the manufacture of lace and straw plait,' but listed only one lace merchant, James Brickwell. His widow, Isabella, is the last lace dealer to appear in a directory in 1830. By then the trade was in serious decline, with prices having been driven down by mechanisation of the process centred on Nottingham. Nevertheless, there were still 152 lace makers working in Amersham in 1851.

Straw Plaiting

Some of the Amersham lace makers responded to declining prices for hand-made lace by turning to

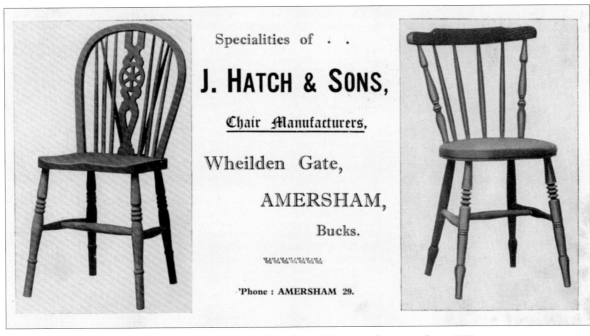

Specialities of . .

J. HATCH & SONS,

Chair Manufacturers,

Wheilden Gate,

AMERSHAM,

Bucks.

'Phone : AMERSHAM 29.

56 An advertisement for Joseph Hatch & Sons, chair manufacturers, about 1935.

57   George Sawyer of Winchmore Hill, with a cart load of chairs bound for London, 1910.

the production of straw plait. The hub of this industry was the growing town of Luton, which had cornered the market in the production of straw hats. Cottagers in the agricultural districts around Luton supplemented their income by weaving split straw into the plait used by the hatters. Amersham was very much on the periphery of the straw plait area, but a small plait market was established at nearby Chesham by 1847. There were 116 plait makers in Amersham in 1851.

Chairmaking

In the early 18th century, it was normal for surplus wood from local beechwoods to be sold to London carpenters, but improvements in road transport enabled local craftsmen to assemble furniture and chairs to sell on the London market. The pioneers of this trade were described in Amersham parish registers as turners, for their skill was in turning chair legs on treadle-operated pole lathes, easily constructed and accommodated in the crudest wooden lean-to. Even larger workshops, where some sort of production line could be arranged, required little investment. Women and children also found employment in making the seats of cane chairs. Lumbering carts, piled high with cheap but durable chairs, set off daily for London. Although the trade never developed to the extent it did in High Wycombe, it did prompt the compiler of *Pigot's Directory* of 1823 to remark that 'considerable employment is found in manufacturing chairs for exportation'. He listed five chairmakers, these being the master craftsmen, who must have employed many more, either on their own premises, or as outworkers.

The 1851 census enables us to find the names of 76 Amersham chairmakers. Typical of these small-scale manufacturers was David Hatch, who set up his chair factory at Hollands Dean, near the *Queens Head Inn*, Whielden Gate, about 1850. The business passed to his son Joseph Hatch, and from him to his son Joseph David Hatch, who was still taking chairs to London on his own cart in the 1920s. The business was sold to the Dunmore Brothers about 1939. The buildings were destroyed by fire in the early 1950s.

Potteries

The clay on the Chiltern plateau is highly suited to the production of bricks, tiles and pottery. It could be dug freely on Amersham Common and Wycombe Heath, where wood to fire the kilns could be easily gathered. The early tile industry around Penn is well documented and high quality, elaborately decorated Penn tiles have been found in many English churches and religious houses. The dissolution of the monasteries reduced the market for decorated floor tiles, but the industry no doubt carried on, serving a more local market. In 1726, William Bovington of Penn insured a tenement in Coleshill, in the occupation of Robert Hailey, potter, with a working shop, kiln house and stable for £100. Coleshill and Winchmore Hill, where most of the Amersham potters lived, were in Hertfordshire and are therefore omitted from the 1798 *Posse Comitatus*. There were, however, three pothawkers listed at nearby Woodrow. The potters carried their stock of domestic earthenware to the neighbouring market towns by pack-horse. By 1851, there were 21 potters at Coleshill and Winchmore

58 One of the last potters to work at Winchmore Hill, photographed in 1909.

Hill, the largest employer being Sarah Slade, of Coleshill Green, who employed five labourers. The trade declined rapidly in the later 19th century, with competition from the Staffordshire potteries and the substitution of cheap ironware for many domestic purposes. A. Morley Davies interviewed a potter at Winchmore Hill in 1909, who worked at the only remaining kiln there but remembered seven pottery kilns operating in the immediate vicinity.[16]

Brickmakers

An examination of the 18th-century fire insurance records for Amersham reveals no thatched houses and only two thatched barns. This was not so much because thatch was a fire hazard, but because the local brick and tile industry had the capacity to meet most householders' and tradesmen's needs. Many of the brick and tile making sites around the town may be ancient, but others, particularly on former common land like Amersham Common and Wycombe Heath, may have been transitory. A few of the sites are described here.

Bryant's map of 1824 shows a brick kiln south of Brentford Wood, on the road to Beaconsfield. This is certainly an old site, for it is listed in Shardeloes rentals from 1739, when it was a tenement and kiln house, let to William Ayres, at £7 10s. per year. William Ayres, brickmaker, paid land tax on the same premises in 1800, but by 1839 they were occupied by James William Woodhams. The nearby place name 'Brickwick' is still on the modern map.

There is still a clay pit at Frog Hall, just south of Upper Bottom Farm. In 1851, this was a brick-works run by Joseph Kirby, who employed eight men there. He was still there in 1881, listed as a brick manufacturer, at Frog Hall Kiln. The brick-works continued until 1975 when a series of photographs was taken by staff of the County Museum.

The first edition Ordnance Survey map of 1880 shows a brickworks on the east side of Cokes Lane, near Snell's Farm. On the 1839 Tithe Map, this part of Snell's Farm is called Great and Little Kiln Field. In 1851, Thomas Andrew, brickmaker, lived at part of Snell's Farm and employed seven men and one boy. In 1891, Albert Saunders, brickmaker, is listed at Snell's Farm.

The 1925 Ordnance Survey map shows a brick-works at the western end of Copperkins Lane, north of Weedon Hill Farm. The was operated by the well-known Amersham builder, George Darlington, whose business premises were at what is now called The Worthies, in the High Street. Known as the Allied Brick and Tile Works, it was still operating as late as 1952.

Amersham International

No review of Amersham's industrial past would be complete without mention of a factory discreetly set up on Amersham Common, early in World War Two. Before the war, Belgium had been the leading producer of natural radium products, using ores mined in its colony in the Congo. A Belgian ship captured by the Royal Navy was found to have such a cargo on board. The government recruited a young chemist named Patrick Grove to use the cargo as the basis of a production unit, with the initial aim of making luminous paint for aircraft instruments. Grove was looking for a site for his factory, not too far from London, but away from the attention of enemy aircraft. In a ministry car, he drove out into the Buckinghamshire country-side, lunched at the *White Lion Inn* and determined to start production at nearby Chilcote House. The government purchased the house and the orchard behind it along Finch Lane, and production continued throughout the war.

In 1945, Patrick Grove realised that there were other uses for radioactive materials and gained ministry approval to expand into new products, such as radium needles for the treatment of cancer. A new company was set up, wholly owned by the government, called the Radiochemical Centre, Amersham. Under Grove's far-sighted leadership, the company attracted some of the best scientists in the field. Further buildings were erected in the orchard behind Chilcote House. The firm quickly became the premier developer of radioactive products for research and medicine in the world. By 1980, it was regularly winning the Queen's Award for Export Achievement and there was a stir in the City of London when the company was privatised. Business grew both at home and overseas, and the company, renamed Amersham International, became Amersham's largest employer. Products developed at the White Lion Road site have revo-lutionised medical diagnosis and genetic research. Much of the work on the analysis of DNA would not have been possible without the company's products and important pharmaceuticals for functional imaging of the heart and brain were developed here.

Five

Turnpike Roads and Coaching Inns

Turnpike Roads

As early as the 16th century, the poor condition of English roads was seen as a great obstacle to economic development. Roads were barely adequate to get produce to local markets, or to the nearest navigable waterway, let alone to act as through routes in themselves. The surfaces were so poor that most goods were carried by pack-horses rather than wagons. In order to promote internal commerce, an Act of 1555 made every parish responsible for the repair of its own roads. Churchwardens appointed surveyors who were to encourage every parishioner to spend up to four days a year working on the roads. In 1563, a further Act increased the number of days to six and made Justices of the Peace responsible for ensuring that parishes fulfilled their obligations. These Acts would place a particular burden on a parish like Amersham, which stood on one of the major roads from London to Birmingham.

There were public coaches using the road through Amersham as early as 1662. In that year, Sir William Dugdale noted in his diary that he travelled 'by Aylesbury Coach'. Coach journeys at that period were so slow that Amersham, being 26 miles from London, may well have been an overnight stop for travellers to the Midlands. Amersham's relative importance as a thoroughfare is shown by a War Office return of beds and stabling available at Buckinghamshire inns in 1686.[1] Aylesbury, as county town, had most beds. Stony Stratford and Fenny Stratford on Watling Street, and Beaconsfield and Wycombe on the Oxford Road, were evidently catering for large numbers of travellers. Buckingham benefited from the traffic between Oxford and Cambridge, but the modest accommodation in Amersham and Wendover suggests that there were far fewer travellers using this third route to the Midlands.

It is quite possible, however, that the 26 beds recorded in Amersham was an under-estimate, as there were at least seven large inns flourishing in the town in 1686. Apart from the *Griffin*, the *Crown*, the *Kings Arms* and the *Swan*, which survive today, there were also the *White Hart* (now known as The Worthies), the *George* (near to the Market House and just west of The Gables) and the original *Saracens Head* (east of the *Griffin* and now 16-22 Broadway). Walter Webb, who kept the *White Hart*, was also a farmer and maltster on a large scale. When he died in 1675, he had 12 beds in the house, plus four truckle beds which slid underneath the larger bedsteads. His property was valued at £1,083, including £65 worth of wheat in the barn and £100 worth of ready-made malt in the malthouse.[2] John Day, who kept the *George Inn* until his death in 1698, had 14 beds including those in his own and his servants' rooms. Guest accommodation was in the 'blue room', the 'matted room,' the chamber over the hall, the chamber over the great parlour, the chamber over the kitchen, and the chamber over the gatehouse.[3] The *White Hart*, the *George*

Town	Beds	Stabling
Aylesbury	101	89
Stony Stratford	100	127
High Wycombe	82	171
Newport Pagnell	77	130
Buckingham	69	177
Beaconsfield	64	64
Fenny Stratford	45	64
Little Brickhill	45	62
Wendover	43	83
Olney	42	63
Winslow	36	87
Marlow	27	44
Amersham	26	51
Chesham	26	44

Beds and Stabling in Buckinghamshire Inns, 1686

(835)

Anno vicefimo quarto

Georgii II. Regis.

An Act for enlarging the Term and Powers granted by Two Acts of Parliament, *For repairing the Road from* Wendover *to the Town of* Buckingham *in the County of* Bucks; and alfo for Repairing and Widening the Road leading from the Weft End of the faid Town of *Wendover* to the End of a Lane called *Oak-Lane,* next the great Road called *The Oxford Road,* lying between the Town of *Beconsfield* in the faid County of *Bucks,* and *Uxbridge* in the County of *Middlefex,* and that Part of the faid great Road which leads from the Weft End of the faid Town of *Beconsfield* to the River *Colne* near *Uxbridge* aforefaid.

𝖂hereas by an Act of 𝖕arliament paſſed in the 𝖘eventh 𝖄ear of the 𝖱eign of 𝖍is late 𝖒ajeſty 𝖐ing George the 𝖋irſt, intituled, An Act for repairing the Road from *Wendover.* to the Town of *Buckingham* in the County of *Bucks;* ſeveral 𝖳olls and 𝖣uties were granted and made payable, and divers 𝖕owers given for repairing the ſaid Road; which ſaid Act, and the 𝖳olls, 𝖣uties, and 𝖕owers thereby granted, were to take 𝖕lace and have 𝖢ontinuance, from the 𝖋ive and twentieth 𝖣ay
Preamble, reciting an Act of 7 Geo. 1.

2   10 B 2   of

59   The road from Wendover to Oak Lane End, near Beaconsfield, was turnpiked by an Act of Parliament passed in 1751.

and the *Saracens Head* were later purchased by the Drake family and became private houses.[4] This may reflect the increased speed of coaches which caused travellers to take their overnight stop much further from London. The coach trade through Amersham may well have declined further when the alternative route to Aylesbury via Berkhamsted became established in the 18th century.

Amersham must have followed with great interest the progress of the Bill which set up the first turnpike on the Great North Road in 1663. This enabled a group of local gentry to charge tolls and apply the proceeds to repairing a 15-mile section of the road passing through several parishes near Royston in Hertfordshire. As the network of turnpike roads grew, regular coaching and carrying services sprang up along the main roads. Ogilby's map of the principal coaching roads, which first appeared in 1675, marks Amersham as 29 miles from London, on the road to the Midlands via Aylesbury, Buckingham and Banbury. Side roads to Wycombe, Beaconsfield and Chesham are shown, leaving the main road in the centre of the town, and the road to Rickmansworth is also shown turning off near the Bury Mill. These maps were available at coaching inns, where they were purchased by wealthy travellers, merchants and carriers. Such a traveller was John Sanders of Chalfont St Peter, who described a journey with his wife to London in 1712. 'She went in the Aylesbury coach, and I on the outside, we dined at the *Crown* at Uxbridge, and went that night to Sir Richard Holford's house in Lincoln's Inn Fields ...'[5]

The first part of the road from London to Birmingham to be turnpiked was the central 20-mile section passing through the difficult clay-lands of the Vale of Aylesbury. An Act of Parliament, passed in 1721, suggested that 'the highway or road leading from Wendover to Buckingham, in the County of Bucks, by reason of the many heavy carriages frequently passing through the same, is become so ruinous and bad, that in the winter season the said road is very dangerous to travellers, and cannot by the ordinary course appointed by the laws and statutes of this realm be repaired'. The Act empowered 51 gentlemen from the north of the county, headed by Ralph Lord Viscount Fermanagh, of Claydon House, to demand tolls from coachmen, wagoners and cattle drovers travelling along the road between Buckingham and Wendover and to apply the receipts to maintaining the road surface.

No similar group of gentry emerged to form a turnpike trust for the section of the road through Amersham, so maintenance of the London Road through the town remained the responsibility of the parish surveyors. Had the road been turnpiked

60 This Wendover to Oak Lane End tollhouse still stands at Great Missenden.

61 This Wendover to Oak Lane End turnpike milestone is still in place on the A413, north-west of Amersham.

in 1720, Montague Garrard Drake would have found it far more difficult to divert its route to the north of the lake he was constructing in Shardeloes Park by damming the River Misbourne. He built a 300-yard section of road from Coldmoreham, crossing the Misbourne on a new bridge and using an old lane west of Mantles Green Farm as the new route to Little Missenden.[6] Stopping up the old highway required the approval of the Quarter Sessions, which accepted that the new road, 40 feet in breadth, would be 'more convenient and commodious to the public'.[7] Parts of the old road can still be followed using the footpath from Coldmoreham, through Shardeloes Park, to Mill End in Little Missenden. The Drakes evidently took less interest in the road to the south of the town for, in 1725, a case was brought at the Quarter Sessions against the inhabitants of Amersham for not repairing the highway between Amersham and Chalfont St Giles.

(535)

Anno octavo

Georgii III. Regis.

An Act for repairing, widening, turning, and altering, the Road leading from *Reading*, in the County of *Berks*, through *Henley*, in the County of *Oxford*, and *Great Marlow, Chipping Wycombe, Agmondesham*, and *Cheynes*, in the County of *Bucks*, and *Rickmansworth, Watford*, and *Saint Albans*, to *Hatfield*, in the County of *Hertford*; and also the Road leading out of the said Road, at *Marlow*, over *Great Marlow Bridge*, through *Bysham*, to or near the Thirty Mile Stone, in the Turnpike Road leading from *Maidenhead* to *Reading*.

WHEREAS the High Road leading Prean from the Town of Reading, in the County of Berks, over Caversham Bridge, by the South Side of Lord Cadogan's Park, through Play-hatch, and to and through the Town of Henley upon Thames, in the County of Oxford, and by Greenland Farm, Mill End, and Medmenham, and to and through the Town of Great Marlow, in the County of Bucks, and by Handy Cross, and to and through the Town of Chipping Wycombe, and over Wycombe Heath, through Wilden Lane, and to and through the Town of Agmon-
6 C 2   desham,

62 The road leading from Reading to Hatfield was turnpiked by an Act of Parliament in 1768.

The next part of the London to Birmingham road to be turnpiked was the 33-mile section from Birmingham, through Warwick, to Warmington, a parish five miles north of Banbury, which was turnpiked in 1726. The Warmington to Buckingham Turnpike Act was passed in 1744 adding a further 22 miles to the route. With the existing Buckingham to Wendover Turnpike, the London to Birmingham road now had turnpike trustees maintaining 75 of its 110 miles.

The missing link in the local turnpike network was put in place by an Act of 1751 which turnpiked

the road leading from the west end of the said town of Wendover to the end of a lane called Oak Lane, next to the great road called the Oxford Road, lying between the town of Beaconsfield in the said County of Bucks, and Uxbridge in the County of Middlesex, and that part of the said great road which leads from the west end of the said town of Beaconsfield to the River Colne near Uxbridge.

The Act claimed that these roads were 'very deep and founderous, and inconvenient and dangerous to persons and carriages passing the same'. The 1751 Act gave responsibility for maintaining these two sections of road to the Buckingham to Wendover Turnpike Trustees, whose numbers were boosted with the addition of over 80 gentlemen from the south of the county, including William Drake and his brother Thomas, Isaac Eeles and the Rev. John Eaton of Amersham. Amongst the Shardeloes Papers are receipts for the subscriptions of William and Thomas Drake towards the cost of repairing and widening the road from Wendover to Oak Lane End in May 1752.

Despite the efforts of the turnpike trustees, carriage of heavy goods by road was still prohibitively expensive. When William Drake was rebuilding Shardeloes in 1758, stone from Headington Quarry was brought by river from Oxford to Spade Oak Wharf near Marlow, and thence by road to Amersham. A consignment of 13 tons of Westmorland slate cost £3 5s. 0d. to bring on the Thames to Eton, whilst it cost a further £6 10s. 0d. to forward it by road to Amersham.[8] There were, however, regular carrying services from Amersham to London, for in 1779 Richard Lee and Edward Smith of Amersham, wagoners, insured their goods in their stables and their barn at Collingwood's Yard, in Amersham, for £300.[9] They also insured their property in a warehouse and stables in the yard of the *Kings Arms Inn*, Holborn Bridge, for £600. Richard Lee was still in business in 1798, when he had 12 horses, three wagons and five carts.

63 A Reading to Hatfield turnpike tollhouse stood on White Lion Road, next to the lodge to Beel House.

The 1751 Turnpike Act was partly repealed by an Act of 1776 which created a new trust to repair the road from Wendover to Oak Lane End. Another trust was to repair the Oxford Road from Beaconsfield to Red Hill, half a mile west of Uxbridge. The remaining half mile into Uxbridge was still to be repaired by the Wendover to Oak Lane End turnpike. This anomaly was not removed until the half mile of road into Uxbridge was added to the Beaconsfield to Red Hill Trust in 1852. Travellers on the Wendover to Oak Lane End road had to pass toll-collector's houses at the west end of Great Missenden and at the bottom of Gravel Hill, Chalfont St Peter. A new toll-collector's house was built at Great Missenden in 1827, and that at Chalfont St Peter was replaced with a new turnpike house at Oak Lane End in 1828. At this time the trustees ceased to employ their own toll-collectors and let all the tolls to William Garlick for £1,000 a year.[10]

The turnpike trustees applied the income from tolls not only to resurfacing the road, but also to improving its route. A major diversion was made in 1828, straightening the road between the 28th and 29th milestones. This improvement bypassed the village of Little Missenden and cut a furlong off the length of the road. Milestones, showing the distance to the major towns, were required by the turnpike acts to be placed along the length of the roads. Most of these inscribed stones on the Wendover to Oak Lane End turnpike are still in place, including the 27th and 28th milestones between the town of Amersham and the parish boundary with Little Missenden.

64 This Reading to Hatfield turnpike milepost, photographed near the *White Lion Inn* about 1930, has since disappeared.

65 A Reading to Hatfield turnpike milepost was sited on the corner of Whielden Street and Broadway. It gave the distance to Hatfield as 24 miles, to Wycombe 7 miles, to Reading 26 miles, and to Rickmansworth 8 miles.

66 This Reading to Hatfield turnpike tollhouse, which stood opposite the *Queens Head* on Whielden Lane, was demolished in 1929.

In the late 18th century, some of the minor cross-country roads were turnpiked. Typical of these was the Reading to Hatfield turnpike, for which an Act was passed in 1768. The road passed through Henley, Marlow, High Wycombe, Amersham, Rickmansworth, Watford and St Albans, but the Act also included an alternative route from the 30th milestone on the Bath Road, across the old wooden bridge over the Thames at Marlow. The Reading to Hatfield Road crossed the Wendover to Oak Lane End turnpike at Amersham, where toll-collector's houses were erected in Whielden Lane and White Lion Road. Two of the distinctive cast-iron mileposts of the Reading to Hatfield Trust are still in place, three and four miles from Amersham, near Chenies. Another stood on the corner of Broadway and Whielden Street, giving the distance to Hatfield as 24 miles and that to Reading as 26 miles. There is a tradition that the Reading to Hatfield road was turnpiked to make it easier for the Cecil family of Hatfield to reach the healing waters and other attractions of the City of Bath. In fact it provided a useful link between several market towns to the north-west of London.

The early turnpike Acts gave trustees powers to charge tolls and to repair the roads for a period of 21 years only. There were four Acts for the Wendover to Oak Lane End road, in 1751, 1776, 1812 and 1833. The last Act, however, extended the trustees' powers for 31 years, plus the period to the end of the parliamentary session then in progress. With the opening of the London to Birmingham Railway in 1838, income from tolls on coaches and carriers' carts declined rapidly. The Wendover to Oak Lane trustees' powers expired in 1865 and the trust was wound up in the following year. The Great Missenden toll-collector's house was sold to Mr. Honnor for £75 and John Hibbert, of Chalfont Park, bought the Oak End turnpike house for £65. The funds still in the treasurer's hands were divided between the parishes which would once again be liable to repair their sections of the road. Amersham and Chalfont St Peter each received £10 17s. 0d. The Reading to Hatfield road remained a turnpike until 1881 and was the last in Buckinghamshire to be disturnpiked. The toll-collector's house at Whielden Lane was demolished for road widening in 1929,[11] whilst the turnpike house on White Lion Road was absorbed into the grounds of Beel House.

67 The original *Saracen's Head* stood on the south side of the Broadway. It can be distinguished by the high carriage entrance and the chimney stack with three diagonal shafts.

68 The *Griffin Inn* has a high coach entrance in the centre. The building was refronted in brick in the early 18th century.

Coaching Inns

The improvement of the road network promoted the development of ever faster and more comfortable coaches. Elizabeth Purefoy of Shalstone, writing to a friend in 1737, informed him that 'the Aylesbury coach goes out from the *Bell Inn* in Holborn every Tuesday at six in the morning and comes to Aylesbury that night, next day it comes to the *Lord Cobham's Arms* at Buckingham ... ' The speed of coaches had evidently increased by 1753, for Henry Purefoy wrote to another family friend that year that 'The Birmingham Coach runs through in a day from London to Buckingham and the fair is ten shillings each passenger.'[12]

Innkeepers along the turnpike roads provided ample accommodation both for travellers and their horses. The inns usually had elegant façades facing the street with tall archways leading to the coach and stable yard. The times at which coach services would call at the inns were well publicised. An ostler would be on hand to replace the horses, whilst the passengers took refreshment during the

69 This interior view of the *Griffin Inn* shows the timber frame and a section of wattle and daub in-filling.

70 The *Crown Inn* is also a timber-framed building, but it was refronted in brick around 1800. The use of large slates enabled the builders to give a less steep angle to the roof and to raise the height of the front bedrooms.

71   The coach entrance and stable yard of the *Crown Inn* in 1912.

72   The fine brick-fronted house with the pediment over the door was the *George Inn*, another of Amersham's old coaching inns.

73 The *King's Arms* had been refronted and the angle of the roof altered about 1800.

fifteen or so minutes allowed for the stop. Establishments which were advertised as 'posting houses' would also hire out horses to pull private coaches to similar inns in the next large town.

Amersham had at least three such inns, the *Griffin*, the *Crown* and the *Kings Arms*. They were all refronted in the late 18th and early 19th centuries, when the coaching trade was at its peak.

74 The coach entrance and stable yard of the *King's Arms* in 1912.

75 By 1930, the *King's Arms* had been redecorated and fake timber framing added to the exterior.

76 In 1936, the timber-framed house to the west was incorporated into the *King's Arms* and the front of the pub was rebuilt to match.

77 Yet another of Amersham's coaching inns was the *White Hart*, which became a private house about 1700. It was more recently the premises of the local builder, George Darlington.

By 1790, the cost of travelling by stage-coach from Amersham to London was 7s. inside, and 3s. 6d. on top of the coach. The Aylesbury to London coach stopped at the *Griffin* every morning at 8 o'clock, whilst the service from London called at the *Griffin* at 2 o'clock each afternoon. The rival Amersham and Missenden coach left the *Crown* at 8 o'clock on the mornings of Monday, Wednesday and Friday, and returned at 6 o'clock in the evening on Tuesday, Thursday and Saturday.[14] The *Crown Inn* was an ancient, timber-framed building, owned by the Drakes of Shardeloes and tenanted at the turn of the 19th century by John Fowler. It was at this time that the front of the *Crown Inn* was rebuilt in brick with sash windows. The brick façade was built up above the old timber framing so that the ceilings of the bedrooms on the front of the inn could be made higher. The new structure was roofed

with Welsh slates, which could be laid at a much more shallow angle than the tiles they replaced.

In the *Posse Comitatus*, John Fowler appears as a victualler in Amersham Town and also features in an appendix as having 10 horses, two wagons and three carts. Fowler employed an ostler to attend to the stage-coach horses and also post-boys, who would ride with the post-horses harnessed to a private coach, or with the post-chaise which he hired to private travellers. His grandson, John Kersley Fowler, ran the *White Hart Inn* in Aylesbury and was the author of three books of recollections of Buckinghamshire life. He tells the story of an elderly gentleman in hunting clothes arriving at the *Crown* and ordering a post-chaise to take him to Windsor. When Tom King, the post-boy, returned with the chaise, he announced that the traveller was none other than King George III.[13] J.K. Fowler

78   The *Swan Inn* was also an early coaching inn. One of the chimneys is dated 1671, but the deeds show that the building is much older.

explained that Tom King was then an old man, for post-boys could in fact be of any age. Their outdoor existence was comparatively healthy and they tended to live to a ripe old age.

With improved roads and superior coach design, travelling times had been reduced dramatically by the 1830s. The *Union*, one of ten coaches belonging to James Hearn & Co., left the *Kings Arms Inn* at Snow Hill in London each day at 8.45 a.m. It went via Ealing and Uxbridge and reached the *Griffin* at Amersham by noon. It stopped at the *Red Lion* at Wendover at 1 p.m. and went on to the *George* in Aylesbury by 2 p.m. The stop at the *Cobham Arms* in Buckingham was at 4 p.m. and the coach completed its 77-mile journey to Banbury by 6 p.m., having averaged over eight miles per hour, including stops for refreshments and fresh horses.

The construction of railways brought a swift end to long-distance coaching. As soon as the London to Birmingham Railway was completed in 1838, coaches were taken off the Holyhead Road as far as Birmingham. The completion of the Great Western line to Bristol in 1841 led to the removal of coaches from the Bath Road. Aylesbury was connected to the London to Birmingham line in 1839 and High Wycombe was reached by a branch from Maidenhead, on the Great Western Railway, in 1854. Stagecoaches were maintained only on routes not yet served by railways. A coach continued to run from Wendover, through Amersham, to London until the 1890s, whilst a horse omnibus also ran from the *Griffin* to the station at Watford. These services survived until in 1892 Amersham itself was connected to the rail network by the Metropolitan Railway.

Six

The Drakes of Shardeloes

Even though the Drake family came from Ashe in Devon, and several sons were given the Christian name Francis, the most creative genealogists have been unable to establish a direct relationship with the Elizabethan mariner, Sir Francis Drake. As minor courtiers, the Drakes increased their family fortune by securing valuable sinecures and marrying wealthy heiresses. The marriage which brought the Drakes to Buckinghamshire took place in 1603, when Francis Drake of Esher, Surrey (a godson of his more famous namesake), married Joan, daughter and co-heir of William Tothill (1557-1626), one of the six Clerks in Chancery and owner of the manor of Weedon Hill in Amersham.

The manor of Weedon Hill, straddling the boundaries of Amersham, Chesham and Little Missenden, had been purchased in 1575 by William Tothill's father Richard, a wealthy printer who held a patent for printing legal books. William Tothill added to his Buckinghamshire estate in 1595 by buying two small properties, adjoining Wycombe Heath, called Woodrow and Shardeloes. These estates had substantial houses on the hillside above Amersham, both of which could be leased to wealthy tenants, but the real value was the unstinted grazing rights on Wycombe Heath and the potential for enclosing more land from the common. William Tothill took up residence at Shardeloes and, in 1624, began negotiations with the Earl of Bedford for the purchase of the main manor of Amersham, with 148 freehold and 25 copyhold tenants.[1] The estate had recently become of much greater value, with the restoration of the right of the burgesses of Amersham to elect two Members of Parliament. This gave the prospective owner the opportunity to influence the outcome of each election. William Tothill lived to see his son-in-law, Francis Drake, elected M.P. for

Amersham in 1625. In his will, William Tothill left £500 to be invested on behalf of the poor of Amersham.

William Drake (1606-69)

William Tothill died in 1626 and was buried at Amersham. His estate at Amersham descended to his grandson, William Drake, who took up residence at Shardeloes and became M.P. for Amersham in 1630. It was this William Drake who, in 1637, completed the purchase of the Borough of Amersham from Francis, Earl of Bedford, for £7,500. The property comprised the manor house of Amersham, called the Bury, then in the tenure of Sir Thomas Saunders, plus several smaller farms, a water corn mill, extensive woodland, and common rights on Amersham Common and Wycombe Heath. As the new lord of the manor, William Drake had the opportunity to control the constant encroachments made by farmers on the perimeter of the two commons. However, it was the Drake family, as lords of the manor, who took in most new land and were the principal beneficiaries when Amersham Common and Wycombe Heath were enclosed by Act of Parliament.

William Drake was created a baronet in 1641, and naturally leaned towards the Royalist cause in the Civil War. His brother, Francis Drake, had married Elizabeth, daughter of the prominent Royalist, Sir Alexander Denton, whose house at Hillesden, near Buckingham, was destroyed by Parliamentary forces in 1643. Although neither brother took an active part in the war, the newspaper *Mercurius Veridicus* reported in 1645 that Shardeloes had been attacked by Parliamentary troops, who had burnt the barns, stables and out-houses, and caused some damage to the house. Sir

79 The Drake family connection with Shardeloes dates from 1603. The park was extended and the lake enlarged by Montague Garrard Drake in 1720.

William Drake and his brother Francis remained MPs for Amersham until Pride's Purge in 1648. It was probably at this time that Sir William Drake decided it was prudent for him to leave the country.

Whilst Sir William Drake was abroad, his affairs were conducted partly by his brother Francis, and partly by his steward at Amersham, James Perrott. There is a surviving three-year lease of Shardeloes, dated 1649, whereby James Perrott was to live in the house and ensure that Sir William's aunt, Catherine Tothill, was provided for. He was also to cultivate the home farm of 160 acres. Amongst the field names given in this lease is Castrupps Close, a 26-acre field later incorporated in Shardeloes Park.[2] This may be part of the hitherto unidentified land and mill at Cattesropp in Amersham, which is listed in the Missenden Abbey cartulary. Indeed Shardeloes may be a later name for Cattesropp and the ornamental lake in the park could well be an enlargement of the old mill pond.

It is not clear how long Sir William Drake spent on the Continent. In 1652, he was appointed to the lucrative government post of Chirographer to the Common Pleas, but this work was almost certainly done by a deputy. He did not stand in the election called by Cromwell in 1654, although his brother Francis was elected as an MP for the County of Surrey. Sir William Drake must surely have been in England in 1657 when the six almshouses he had endowed were built in Amersham High Street. With the Restoration of Charles II, Sir William Drake again represented Amersham in Parliament and, in 1662, Sir William Drake bought the rectory of Amersham from Sir Richard Minshull for £1,100.[3] Although the rectory did not become vacant during his lifetime, the purchase enabled his successors to nominate members of the Drake family as rectors of Amersham. The Drakes, as squires, Members of Parliament and rectors, were thus in a position to dominate the town. Sir William Drake died

80 Amersham's fine Market Hall was erected by Sir William Drake in 1682. It is decorated with his coat of arms and initials. His descendant, William Wykeham Tyrwhitt-Drake, restored the building in 1911.

unmarried in 1669, leaving his Amersham estate to his brother's son William Drake.

There is a lengthy epitaph to Sir William Drake on his monument in Amersham church. It describes him as a model student at Oxford, a collector of valuable books, and an avid reader until the failure of his eyesight in later life. It explains how he inherited great wealth, paid off his father's debts and gave the family estate in Surrey to his brother. In rather obscure Latin, the epitaph goes on to justify his conduct during the Civil War, when he remained 'faithful to the King and obedient to the Church, when these very things were in the order of a crime. He hated the wicked struggles of the rebels and escaped unharmed because of his sense of duty and his good sense … at home he escaped by being prudent and abroad he escaped by being absent … He not only saved the wealth of his grandfather by these arts, but even increased it … and following the example of his grandfather, did much good to the poor.'[4]

William Drake (1651-90)

William Drake, who inherited the Amersham estate from his uncle in 1669, was the son of Francis Drake by his second wife, Dorothy, daughter of Sir William Spring, of Pakenham, Suffolk. William Drake became MP for Amersham in 1669 and remained in Parliament until his death in 1690. He made a very advantageous marriage to Elizabeth, daughter and heir of Sir William Montague, Lord Chief Baron of the Court of Exchequer. He is best known in Amersham as the builder of the Market Hall in the middle of the High Street, which bears the initials WD and the date 1682. He died in 1690 and is buried at Amersham.

Montague Drake (1673-98)

On the death of William Drake in 1690, the Amersham estate passed to his son Montague, who represented Amersham in Parliament from 1695. He was reputed to be one of the handsomest

81 William Drake built the present house at Shardeloes between 1758 and 1767.

men of his generation and married another heiress, Jane, daughter of Sir John Garrard, Bart., of Lamer, near Hatfield. His sister, Mary Drake, also made a valuable alliance when she married Sir John Tyrwhitt, Bart., of Stainfield in Lincolnshire. The Lincolnshire property later descended to the Drakes of Amersham when the male line of the Tyrwhitt family died out. Montague Drake was injured falling from his horse whilst riding at night from London and never fully recovered. He died in 1698 at the early age of 25 and was buried at Amersham, where there is a fine monument to him in the chancel. There is a lengthy inventory of his goods, both at his house in London and at Shardeloes, where the contents of over 50 rooms are carefully listed. The valuation extends to the crops growing on the home farm, including

six acres of beans and peas, worth £10 10s. 0d. growing at Little Castrope.[5]

Montague Garrard Drake (1692-1728)
When Montague Drake died in 1698, the heir to the Amersham estate was his six-year-old son, Montague Garrard Drake. Whilst he was under the guardianship of his mother Jane, he was educated at home by a succession of tutors. He went up to Oxford at the age of 13, and on the Grand Tour in 1710. During this time, his uncle, John Drake, occupied one of the Amersham seats in Parliament. Montague Garrard Drake married, in 1719, Isabella, daughter and heir of Thomas Marshall, a wealthy London merchant. When he entered Parliament as Member for Amersham, in 1713, he supported the Tory party. From 1722 to 1727 he was one of the

82 After the death of the original architect, Stiff Leadbetter, William Drake employed Robert Adam to complete his new house. Adam designed the huge portico at Shardeloes.

Buckinghamshire representatives, and from 1727 until his death he held the Amersham seat again.

Montague Garrard Drake added greatly to the Drake family holding in Amersham. He bought the freehold of several houses and business premises, including the *Swan Inn* in 1722, the *George Inn* near the Market House in 1723, and the *Saracens Head* in the Broadway in 1724. These purchases increased the number of substantial tenants who could be relied upon to support the Drake family candidates at election time. He also began the process of improving and enlarging Shardeloes to match the wealth and position in society which the Drake family had attained. He was evidently impressed by the art of landscape gardening for, in 1720, he paid for the diversion of the London Road to the north side of the Misbourne valley so that Shardeloes lake

could be enlarged. In 1722, he began building a range of domestic offices and stables which still stand to the west of Shardeloes House. He later employed the Venetian architect, James Leoni, who was then working on Clandon Park in Surrey, to prepare 'several sketches for the four new fronts of Shardeloes House'. Montague Garrard Drake died of gout at Bath in 1728 before any further work on Shardeloes could commence. His lavish lifestyle had led him to take out a series of loans and mortgages which his successors had to pay off. There is a large monument to him in the Drake Chapel in Amersham church.

William Drake (1723-96)

Montague Garrard Drake was succeeded by his seven-year-old son William. William Drake married, in 1747, Elizabeth, daughter and heiress of John Raworth, a director of the South Sea Company.[6] This injection of cash enabled William Drake to rebuild Shardeloes completely between 1758 and 1766 at a cost of £19,000. The original architect was Stiff Leadbetter of Eton, who envisaged a square house with towers at each corner. Robert Adam subsequently took over the contract, deleting the towers and substituting the large portico on the north side. William Drake appointed his brother, Thomas Drake, as rector of Amersham in 1753. On the death of Thomas in 1775, William appointed his son, John Drake, to succeed him at the rectory. William Drake paid for the repairs to Amersham church and rectory undertaken by the architect Samuel Wyatt between 1775 and 1785.[7]

William Drake was returned as MP for Amersham in 1746. He held the seat until his death in 1796, but there is no record of his ever having made a speech in the House of Commons. His eldest son, William Drake (1747-95), sat as Member of Parliament for Amersham from 1768 until his death. He, in contrast, spoke frequently in Parliament, generally advocating caution in public expenditure. He was described by the Public Ledger as 'a very independent, conscientious man, votes on each side but most usually in the minority'. William Drake the younger married two heiresses. The first was Mary, daughter and heiress of William Hussey, MP for Salisbury. She died in 1778. He then married, in 1781, Rachel Elizabeth, daughter and heiress of Jeremiah Ives of Norwich. The *Gentleman's Magazine*, reporting his death in 1795, stated that 'He has left an immense property partly acquired by marriage, and partly by some collateral branches. Had he lived to inherit that of his father, he would have been one of the richest men in the country.'

Thomas Drake Tyrwhitt-Drake (1749-1810)

When William Drake the elder died in 1796, his heir was his second son, Thomas. Born in 1749, he had changed his name to Thomas Drake Tyrwhitt in order to inherit property in Lincolnshire, bequeathed to him in the will of Sir John de la Fontaine Tyrwhitt, Bart., proved in 1761. On inheriting the Amersham estate in 1796, he obtained royal licence to change his name back again to Drake. He and his younger brother John Drake (1756-1826), rector of Amersham, married two sisters who were co-heirs of the Rev. William Wickham, of Garsington in Oxfordshire. Thomas Drake Tyrwhitt-Drake continued the policy of purchasing the freeholds of property in Amersham. He bought the valuable Hyrons Farm, adjacent to Amersham Common, from William Morten in 1808,[7] and was elected MP for Amersham in 1796, retaining the seat until his death in 1810. He was succeeded by his son Thomas Tyrwhitt-Drake.

Thomas Tyrwhitt-Drake (1783-1852)

Thomas Tyrwhitt-Drake appears to be the first of the family obsessed with fox hunting. This was always a costly pastime and one which diverted the Drakes from the necessary care of their estates. More importantly, perhaps, it led to their being attracted to women who were good riders rather than wealthy heiresses. Thomas Tyrwhitt-Drake and his brother John, whom he appointed rector of Amersham in 1826, married daughters of Arthur Annesley of Blechingdon, Oxfordshire. Thomas Tyrwhitt-Drake maintained a hunting estate at Bucknell, near Bicester, and was Master of the Bicester Hounds from 1830 to 1851.

Thomas Tyrwhitt-Drake was a Member of Parliament for Amersham from 1805 until the town was disenfranchised by the 1832 Reform Act. He rarely attended the House of Commons. His brother, William Tyrwhitt-Drake, was a serving cavalry officer who fought at the Battle of Waterloo. He was the first Chairman of Amersham Board of Guardians in 1835. He occupied the second Amersham seat in the House of Commons from 1810 to 1832. When called upon to vote on an important motion in 1812, William Tyrwhitt-Drake said that his brother would not be in town and supposed that he was hunting in Oxfordshire. Thomas Tyrwhitt-Drake was Sheriff of Buckinghamshire in 1836. He is said to have opposed the building of the London to Birmingham Railway along the Misbourne valley as it would spoil his view from Shardeloes. He died at Bucknell in 1852 and was succeeded by his eldest son, Thomas Tyrwhitt-Drake.

83 The Old Berkeley Hunt, near Shardeloes Lake, about 1920.

Thomas Tyrwhitt-Drake (1817-88)

Thomas Tyrwhitt-Drake shared his father's passion for fox hunting and was Master of Bicester Hounds from 1852 to 1855, 1857 to 1862 and 1863 to 1866. He built kennels for the Bicester Hounds at Stratton Audley. He also provided kennels at Shardeloes when his cousin, Thomas Henry Tyrwhitt-Drake, of Little Shardeloes, a captain in the Indian Army, formed a new pack to hunt the western side of Old Berkeley Hunt in 1888. Thomas Tyrwhitt-Drake married, in 1843, Elizabeth Julia, widow of Col. Wedderburn and daughter of John Stratton, of Turweston House, near Buckingham. He was Sheriff of Buckinghamshire in 1859. Although his father had opposed the building of the railway through the Misbourne valley in the 1830s, Thomas Tyrwhitt-Drake, in 1887, sold land for the building of the Metropolitan Railway across Amersham Common. He died in 1888 and was succeeded by his son, Thomas William Tyrwhitt-Drake.

Thomas William Tyrwhitt-Drake (1849-1900)

Thomas William Tyrwhitt-Drake was also a hunting squire and assisted his cousin, Captain Drake, as Master of the western division of Old Berkeley. He married, in 1874, Frances Anne Isabella, daughter of Col. Robert Algernon Smith-Dorrien, of Haresfoot, Hertfordshire. On the death of Thomas William Tyrwhitt-Drake in 1900, the Amersham estate passed to his brother William Wykeham Tyrwhitt-Drake.

William Wykeham Tyrwhitt-Drake (1851-1919)

William Wykeham Tyrwhitt-Drake was described as 'a bold and brilliant rider to hounds and a fair shot … what delights him most is hunting and shooting, at both of which he is an enthusiastic expert'.[8] In 1902, he became Master of the Old Berkeley West Hounds, for which he provided kennels at Shardeloes. He then hunted for three years with the Bicester Hunt before resuming as Master of the Old Berkshire Hounds from 1905 to

84 This fine brick house at the west end of Amersham is called Little Shardeloes. Its origin is not known, but the Drake family used it as a dower house, or leased it to wealthy individuals like William Bent, who lived there until his death in 1699.

1909 and from 1913 to 1914. His hunting commitments were to some extent underwritten by sales of hundreds of building plots, laid out on those parts of Hyrons Farm which were nearest the new railway station. He was responsible for the restoration of Amersham's Market Hall in 1911. William Wykeham Tyrwhitt-Drake married Augusta, daughter of the Rev. Herbert Richard Peel, of Thornton Hall, near Buckingham. He died in 1919 and was succeeded by his son Edward Thomas Tyrwhitt-Drake.

Edward Thomas Tyrwhitt-Drake (1887-1933)
Edward Thomas Tyrwhitt-Drake carried on the family tradition of devoting their lives to fox hunting. He was Master of the Old Berkeley Hunt from 1921 to 1931. He was Sheriff of Buckinghamshire in 1927. In 1928, Edward Tyrwhitt-Drake was forced to sell a large part of his property in the town of Amersham, including the *Griffin*, the *Crown* and the *Swan* inns. He married Venice Marguerite, daughter of Uvedale Bennett Corbett, of Crabwall Hall, Cheshire, but had no male heir. He was succeeded by his cousin, Thomas Tyrwhitt-Drake, the son of Guy Percival Tyrwhitt-Drake (1859-1928), a younger brother of William Wykeham Tyrwhitt-Drake.

Thomas Tyrwhitt-Drake (1893-1956)
Thomas Tyrwhitt-Drake was born at Heyshott, Sussex. He fought in the Great War with the 52nd Battalion Oxford and Bucks Light Infantry and twice won the Military Cross in 1916. Whilst serving in Iraq in 1924, he was injured in a hunting accident and was paralysed from the waist down. He inherited Shardeloes in 1933, in which year he married Philomena, daughter of Col. Edward Mostyn of Tower House, Arundel, Sussex. They were the last of the Tyrwhitt-Drake family to live at Shardeloes. In 1939, the house was requisitioned as a maternity hospital to which expectant mothers from London were brought each week. About 3,000 children were born there during the war. Shardeloes remained empty after the war and was threatened with demolition. It was finally sold for conversion into luxury flats in 1958. Thomas Tyrwhitt-Drake lived instead at Little Shardeloes, where he died in 1956. The remaining Amersham property passed to his brother, Francis Tyrwhitt-Drake, who moved to Bereleigh House, East Meon, Hampshire. His son, William Tyrwhitt-Drake, is the present occupant of that house. He is well-known in Hampshire as a keen sportsman and a strong supporter of the Countryside Alliance. He remains the lord of the manor of Amersham to this day.

Seven

Churches and Chapels

Amersham Franchise

It was customary in the medieval period for great landowners to found abbeys, priories and nunneries, to demonstrate their piety and to ensure that a substantial number of priests would pray for their immortal souls. Geoffrey de Mandeville, the first Earl of Essex, founded Walden Abbey, near Saffron Walden, in 1140. In order to provide a steady income to the abbey, he made over to the abbot a large portfolio of land in several counties, including the glebe land of Amersham and the right to appoint a priest there. The glebe land included valuable meadow land either side of the River Misbourne. Its alienation to a distant

85 Prior to its Victorian restoration, St Mary's Church was entirely rendered over with cement, concealing the differences in age of the masonry of the various aisles and chapels, which had, over the centuries, been added to the medieval building.

86 Amersham's nonconformists can trace their origins back before the Reformation, to when many local men and women offended the church authorities by reading the Bible in English and presuming to form their own religious views. This memorial was erected near Rectory Wood in 1931, near to the place where, tradition has it, six of their number were burnt at the stake in 1521.

abbey, sixty years before a market charter was obtained and the Borough of Amersham was laid out, explains why some of the houses on the north side of the High Street are not in the borough. These houses, stretching from the east end of Turpins Row, to the former *Red Lion Inn*, plus the brewery and the houses in Church Street, were always reckoned as part of 'Amersham Franchise', as the occupants had no vote in borough elections.

Tithes

The most valuable element of church property was, of course, the right to collect tithes. Tithes were a tenth of the crop of all farmers, collected by the priest at harvest time and used to feed his own family and to maintain the parish church. Given the huge acreages of wheat and barley grown in Amersham, the tithes were a very valuable asset. The Abbot of Walden, had he followed the practice of most religious houses, would have appointed a poorly paid vicar to attend to the spiritual needs of the parish, whilst the tithe income was used to support the Abbey. Although he did nominate some of the earliest known priests at Amersham, the records of Pope Nicholas's ecclesiastical taxation of 1291 show that the Abbot was receiving only £3 6s. 8d. per year from Amersham. The Earl of Essex had evidently taken back the right to collect the tithes and no doubt his appointee as rector enjoyed the tithe income himself. The rectory of Amersham was thereafter a highly sought after preferment, in the gift of the lord of the manor of Amersham.

Religious Dissent

Although the tithes of Amersham could be expected to attract able and ambitious priests to the town, successive rectors failed to meet the spiritual needs of the population. Even before the Reformation, Amersham gained a reputation for independence of thought, with several local tradesmen appearing before church courts, accused of denying key doctrines of the Catholic church. They were perhaps encouraged by the Cheyne family, lords of the manor of Chesham Bois, who shared their views and tended to appoint radical priests to serve in the church there. The names of several Amersham men who were burnt at the stake, in 1506 and in 1521, for little more than daring to read the Bible in their own language, are inscribed on a stone column, erected near Rectory Wood in 1931. News of their persecution merely encouraged others to read the Bible and work out their own salvation. Even after the establishment of the Church of England under Henry VIII and its refinement under Edward VI and Elizabeth I, there were many puritans in the Amersham area who felt that the English church had not distanced itself enough from those elements of Catholic doctrine and liturgy which were repellent to them.

Appointing the Rector

At the beginning of the 17th century, the manor and rectory of Amersham belonged to Edward Russell, 3rd Earl of Bedford. The rector was Robert Challoner, founder of Amersham Grammar School. A Russell family settlement resulted in the rectory passing to Anne, grand-daughter of the 2nd Earl of Bedford, who was married to a Catholic, Henry Lord Herbert. Henry later succeeded his father as Earl of Worcester and was one of the principal financiers of the King during the Civil War. In 1617, Henry Lord Herbert entered into an agreement with John and Henry Croke, sons of John Croke of Chilton in Buckinghamshire, that their brother Charles Croke would be appointed rector of Amersham should Robert Challoner vacate the rectory.[1] The Crokes, if not themselves Catholics, were linked by marriage to the Blounts and the Dormers, two of the most prominent Catholic families in the county. When Robert Challoner died in 1624, Charles Croke was therefore appointed rector of Amersham by a leading Catholic aristocrat. If the local puritans knew of this arrangement, they would have been as suspicious of their new rector as they were when King Charles I took a Catholic wife. If they knew that, in 1638, Edward Lord Herbert, the son of Henry Earl of Worcester, sold the rectory of Amersham to the known Catholic, Sir Richard Minshull, they would have felt even more betrayed. Sir Richard Minshull's house at Bourton, near Buckingham, was burnt down in August 1642, within days of his declaring for the King at the outbreak of the English Civil War.

The Civil War

Charles Croke's family background and the nature of his appointment to the rectory of Amersham would have been a deep embarrassment in 1642, when the nation stumbled into Civil War. Amersham was a staging post on the road from London to the Parliamentary garrison at Aylesbury. Neremiah Wharton, a Parliamentary soldier, wrote from Aylesbury in August 1642, that he had brought amunition, bound for Aylesbury, through Amersham, 'which is the sweetest country I ever saw, and as is the country so also is the people'. Wharton reports that at Hillingdon his fellow soldiers had ripped up the priest's surplices for handkerchiefs and at

Uxbridge had burned the hated communion rails. If they had found similar popish symbols in Amersham, they too would have been destroyed.[2]

Two of the leading Royalists in the town, Sir Thomas Saunders and his brother Francis, who held the lease of the Bury Farm, were forced to pay a hefty fine by the Parliamentarians. Had the rector of Amersham not accommodated his own views to those of the local puritans and the zealous soldiers passing through the town, he would surely have been ejected in the first years of the war, let alone in 1646, when Cromwell sacked the bishops and tried to make the Church of England Presbyterian. Charles Croke's survival is all the more remarkable, as his brother Henry, then living at Chequers, and his nephew John, at Chilton, were both forced to pay heavy fines for their adherence to the Royalist cause. Charles Croke supplemented his income as rector of Amersham by tutoring wealthy young men. There is an elegant memorial in Amersham church to one such pupil, Henry Curwen, who died at Amersham in 1636. Charles Croke was still at the rectory in December 1650, when Vere Bertie, son of Lord Willoughby, left Amersham 'because the Doctor has given over school'. In 1654, Charles Croke gave up the struggle to hold on to the rectory of Amersham and, probably under duress, recommended a young puritan called Edward Terry as his replacement.[3] He retired to Feathard, Tipperary, where Cromwell had so recently crushed Irish Royalist and Catholic opposition. Charles Croke died in County Carlow in 1657. Edward Terry was then confirmed as rector of Amersham. Terry was succeeded in 1659 by the Rev. John Phillips, but he was one of the many Presbyterian ministers ejected at the Restoration of Charles II, when a traditional Church of England priest, the Rev. Thomas Crawley, was appointed rector of Amersham.

This strange chapter in Amersham's church history closes in 1662, when Sir Richard Minshull, with his former possessions restored to him by a grateful Charles II, sold the manor of the rectory of Amersham to Sir William Drake for £1,100. However, the freedom of worship enjoyed in Amersham during the interregnum could not be withdrawn so easily. The former Presbyterian rector, Edward Terry, returned to the district, living in Chalfont St Giles

87 The rectory was rebuilt about 1732, during the incumbency of the Rev. Benjamin Robertshaw, who died there in 1744. It was further embellished by Samuel Wyatt, when working at Shardeloes and St Mary's church between 1775 and 1785.

at the home of widow Fleetwood, which was registered as a dissenters' meeting house in 1672. On the other side of the town, George Swinho, the ejected Presbyterian minister of St Leonards, had purchased Woodrow High House and this too was registered as a meeting house in 1672.

Rev. Benjamin Robertshaw

The Rev. Benjamin Robertshaw was appointed rector by William Drake in 1728. He found that the court of the manor of Amersham rectory had not been held for many years. He drew up a list of those who should have been paying the rector a chief rent on their property, including Mary Ball, who paid a chief rent of 2s. 11d. on Amersham Brewery, and John Hunt, maltster, who paid 2s. 6d. for his house, which survives today as Amersham Museum.[4] These courts continued to be held into the 19th century, when these small sums became too expensive to collect.

Benjamin Robertshaw was an unusually diligent and capable rector. He rebuilt the neglected rectory in 1732. Robertshaw was well aware how recently the rector's privileged position had been under threat. In a marginal note in the parish registers, he gave his own verdict on the characters who dominated Amersham during the Civil War. 'General Fleetwood lived at the Vache, and Russell on the opposite hill, and Mrs Cromwell, Oliver's wife, and her daughters, at Woodrow High House, where afterwards lived Capt. James Thompson; so the whole country was kept in awe, and became exceedingly zealous, and very fanatical, nor is the poison yet eradicated, but the Whartons are gone, and the Hampdens a-going.' He referred in particular to the Parliamentary General, George Fleetwood, a signatory to Charles I's death warrant, and to Sir Francis Russell, a justice of the peace who performed civil marriages in Amersham during the Commonwealth.

88 Although the Quakers were using part of an orchard on Whielden Street as a burial ground as early as 1665, fear of persecution prevented them from building their Meeting House on the site, at least until 1689.

The Friends Meeting House

The suspension of royal and church courts during the Civil War freed political and religious activists to publish and preach whatever they liked. A large measure of freedom remained under the Commonwealth, but even Oliver Cromwell must have been horrified to read the pamphlet entitled *Good News from Buckinghamshire*, which contained positively socialist ideals. In 1653, two Amersham tradesmen, Andrew Burrows, a clothier, and Edward Perrott, a maltster, were accused of posting up in the market house scandalous papers leading to the disturbance of the peace.[5] The puritans of Amersham were free to interpret the scriptures in whatever way they thought fit, and whilst they struggled with the rector, Charles Croke, over the direction the parish church should take, two separate religious groups emerged, the most powerful initially being the Quakers. Even after the restoration of Charles II, and the introduction

of new penalties to suppress religious dissent, the local Quakers worshipped openly, led by Isaac Pennington, who leased the Bury Farm, and Thomas Ellwood, who lived in Coleshill. They enjoyed the support of many wealthy tradesmen such as Edward Perrott, whose eventful funeral in 1665 was described by Thomas Ellwood:

> When as the body was being borne on Friends shoulders along the street in order to be carried to the burying ground, which was at the town's end, being part of an orchard belonging to the deceased ...; Ambrose Benett [of Bulstrode] a barrister at law and Justice of the Peace ... rushed out of his inn with his constables and a rabble of rude fellows and having his drawn sword in his hand struck one of the foremost bearers with it, commanding them to set down the coffin. Enraged by their delay, Benett set his hand on the coffin and threw it to the ground in the open street and in the cartway, so that all the travellers that passed by (whether horsemen, coaches, carts or wagons) were fain to break out of the way to go by it, that

they might not drive over it. The body was later buried in an unconsecrated part of the churchyard. The Friends were taken before Benett and another J.P. at the Griffin Hotel, ten of them being committed to the Gaol at Aylesbury.[6]

When an enquiry was made in 1669 as to the strength of nonconformity in the diocese, it fell to John Stoning, curate of Amersham, to admit to the bishop that the non-conformists in Amersham were very active. He professed to know little of the dissenters, but mentioned Mr. Swinho preaching to the Presbyterians at his house at Woodrow. He also noted:

> Quakers, these meet mostly at an house called The Berry, it is Isaac Pennington's house, who is commonly their speaker. These have so met ever since I came to this place, which is two years since. There are of them as I heard sometimes almost two hundred at a time, but most of the poorest sort.[7]

Amersham's Quakers were vigorously persecuted by the authorities until the 'Glorious Revolution' of 1688. In 1689, part of Joseph Winch's house in Whielden Street was registered as a Quaker meeting house. This may have been the southern part of the building still in use today as a meeting house. This measure of freedom did not, however, satisfy local Quakers. In 1706, four of their leaders, John Pennington of Beel House, Thomas Ellwood of Coleshill and Abraham Butterfield and William Catch, refused to pay their tithes and were taken to court by Joshua Leaper, the bailiff of Montague Garrard Drake of Shardeloes, who also collected the tithes on behalf of the rector, Humphrey Drake. It took three years to resolve the case, which ended with the sequestration of the defendants' goods to the value of the unpaid tithes.[8] This may have been a test case, and it is highly likely that more local Quakers, having endured years of persecution and made great personal sacrifice to build their own place of worship, should take a stand against the payment of tithes to the Church of England. In response to another enquiry from the bishop in 1709, the curate, Benjamin Robertshaw, had to admit that one third of the population of Amersham were dissenters, with 90 attending the Quaker meeting house each Sunday.[9]

It is not difficult to account for the rapid decline of the Quaker congregation in Amersham in the 18th century. The founders' high moral standards were too demanding for many of their successors, and the practice of vetting members' marriage partners must have dramatically limited the choice of young Quakers. Only three Amersham Quakers are listed in the *Posse Comitatus* in 1798. By 1851, the Friends Meeting House was in the care of John Impey, who occupied Quarrenden Mill. He filled in the return for the religious census which coincided with the population census of that year. He had to admit that there were only two people in the congregation, probably himself and his wife, and that the average attendance was also two.[10] The meeting house was soon after let to the Methodists and only re-opened as a Quaker meeting house in 1917.

The Upper Meeting House

In 1669, the curate, John Stoning, reported that a group of Anabaptists had been meeting for at least two years at the house of David Jameson at Woodside. He named Robert Turner, a maltster in the town, and Edward Redrup, a blacksmith, as their teachers. By 1675, when the group's first register of baptisms and burials commences, they were meeting at the house of Henry Pratt. In 1676, Pratt and Redrup purchased from another member of the group, Thomas Charsley, a part of his orchard, between the High Street and the Common Plat, for use as a burial ground. Robert Turner was one of the first to be buried there in 1677. When Henry Pratt gave notice that he could no longer risk prosecution for holding the meetings in his house, the group decided to build a meeting house on the burial ground. David Jameson headed a list of 26 members who contributed to the building fund in 1677.[11] By 1709, about 70 members were attending services at the Baptist meeting house each Sunday.

In the 1720s, Amersham's Baptists had to face up to an issue which had split the Baptist Church nationally. Those believing in the possibility that all men were redeemable decided to join the General Baptist Association, whilst the remainder, who believed in predestination and the redemption of a select few, set up a separate Particular Baptist congregation. The General Baptists continued to

89 The General Baptists in Amersham were bold enough to build a meeting house in an orchard off the High Street in 1677. The present building was put up on the same site in 1779 and is now a private house.

worship at the old meeting house behind the *King's Arms* in the High Street. It was probably in response to the opening of a rival meeting of Particular Baptists in premises next door, that a new meeting house was built in 1779. The new building, financed by a leading member called John Harding, became known as the Upper Meeting House, to distinguish it from the adjacent Particular or 'Lower Meeting House'.

Despite building their new meeting house, the General Baptists declined in numbers and the Upper Meeting House was taken over in 1823 by yet another group of Baptists who had broken away from the Lower Meeting House. On that rainy morning in March 1851, when a national census of religious attendance was held, 88 people made their way to the Upper Meeting House. The building still survives, but has been a private house since 1944.

90   The Particular Baptists built what was to become known as the Lower Baptist Meeting House in the garden of the minister, Richard Morris, in 1784.

91   The Methodists, who for many years held their services at the old Friends Meeting House in Whielden Street, built their own church on the High Street in 1899.

92 St Mary's Church was radically altered in 1871, when the architect Frederick Preedy was employed to modernise the interior. The box pews and galleries were removed, the three-decker pulpit was replaced and the chancel arch was heightened.

The Lower Meeting House

Following the schism in the 1720s, when many of the congregation joined the General Baptist movement, the remainder withdrew and formed a Particular Baptist church. They may well have met at the home of a sawyer called John Bigg, whose house at Woodrow was licensed as a meeting house in 1725. In 1734, he leased a building plot at Woodrow to 13 trustees for the erection of a permanent meeting house.[12] There must have been a burial ground attached to this meeting house for, from 1741, the rector of Amersham began to note burials of Baptists at Woodrow in the registers of the parish church. The Particular Baptists at Woodrow were taught by a Mr. Harris. When he became too old and infirm to carry on, the group invited a newcomer, Richard Morris, to be their pastor.

Richard Morris came to Amersham in 1775. He was a charismatic figure who had been discharged from the army after refusing to attend church parades. Within months of his arrival in the town, he was selected as pastor to the Particular Baptists at Woodrow. Soon afterwards, he married Sarah Hobbs, a leading member of the General Baptist congregation, and set up home in her house next door to the old meeting house. As if this were not provocative enough, he converted a workshop in his back yard into a meeting house for Particular

Baptists and replaced this with a brand new building in 1784. In 1792, his flock at Woodrow abandoned their meeting house there and joined the Particular Baptists in the town. Morris further extended what had now become known as the Lower Meeting House in 1799. After the alterations, it measured 45 ft. square and seated 700.[13] By the time Richard Morris died in 1817, his Particular Baptist congregation was flourishing, whilst the neighbouring General Baptist congregation at the Upper Meeting House was in terminal decline. When it was decided in 1842 to build a British School for the children of Amersham's nonconformists, the school was added to the back of the Lower Meeting House. In March 1851, no fewer than 435 people attended the morning service there. The Lower Meeting House is still thriving and the interior was completely refurbished in 1980.

The Methodist Church

In a town dominated by two Baptist churches, it is not surprising that the Methodist Church, a much later secession from the Church of England, struggled to gain a foothold. It was probably under the direction of the local doctor, Thomas Nathaniel Gray, who came to live at Apsley House on the High Street in the 1820s, that the small group of Methodists in the town became a force to be

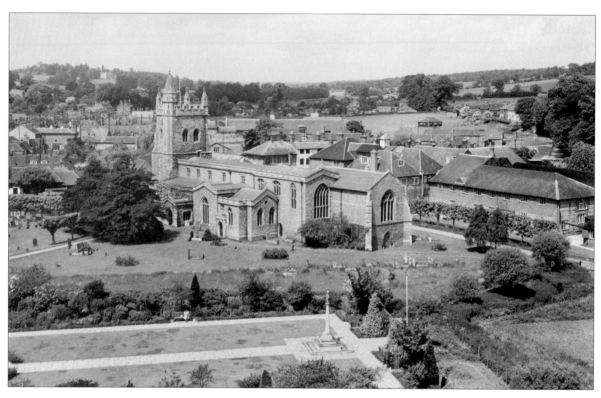

93 The architectural history of St Mary's Church was further obscured by a restoration begun in 1889, when the entire structure was re-faced in knapped flint with ashlar stone dressings. The tower was also rebuilt and the octagonal staircase topped with a spirelet.

reckoned with. On 30 March 1851, Dr. Gray reported that 23 members attended the morning service at the converted cottage at Bury End, then used by the Methodists. When Dr. Gray moved to London in 1860, the Methodists rented the former Friends Meeting House in Whielden Street. They stayed at Whielden Street until 1899, when the present church was built on the site of Andrew Lane's Almshouses, opposite the *Swan Inn*.

The Restoration of St Mary's Church

The Church of England eventually responded to the challenge of nonconformity. The 19th century saw renewed energy and a change of style in the established church. This was reflected locally in the removal of the Archdeaconry of Buckingham from the huge Diocese of Lincoln in 1837, and its addition to the Diocese of Oxford. The change was not made effective until the appointment in 1845 of Samuel Wilberforce as the new Bishop of Oxford.

Wilberforce opposed the holding of the religious census in 1851, despite the fact that it proved the strength of nonconformity across the nation and therefore the need for reform of the established church which he advocated. Wilberforce took a particular interest in church buildings and encouraged parishes to modernise their churches. The prevailing style was gothic, harking back to the perceived medieval purity of a unified church.

In Amersham, the rector, the Rev. Edward Tyrwhitt-Drake, set about the restoration of St Mary's Church in 1871. He employed Frederick Preedy, a well-respected church architect and designer of stained glass, to overhaul completely the interior of the church.[14] The emphasis of church services was moving away from the sermon towards the liturgy, so the three-decker pulpit was removed and the chancel arch was raised to enhance the view of the altar and the fine east window. The boxed pews and galleries were

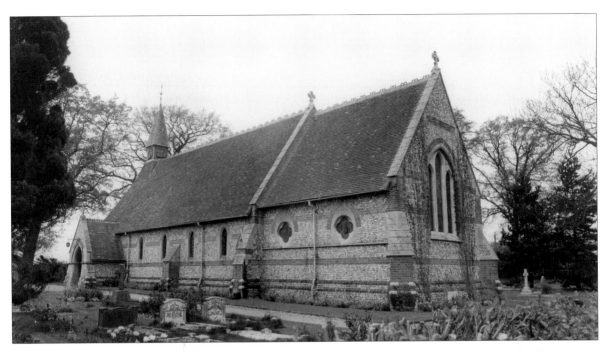

94 A new church was built to serve the hamlet of Coleshill in 1860. It was designed by George Street, the architect of the recently formed Diocese of Oxford.

95 St Mary's Mission Church was built on White Lion Road in 1907, using materials from an old railway contractor's hut. The brick and corrugated-iron structure lasted until 1935.

96 St George's Church was built in 1935 to replace St Mary's Mission Church.

97 St George's Church was designed to be extended at a later date. The arcading in the nave was intended to give access to spacious side aisles.

98 St Michael's Mission Church began in a temporary building on Sycamore Road in 1920. The present church was built on the same site in 1966.

removed and replaced with open benches, more akin to the ones the restorers thought medieval worshippers might have sat upon. The clear glass which had let in light in an age of reason was replaced with devotional stained glass designed by Preedy.

The Rev. Edward Tyrwhitt-Drake raised more funds in 1889 for a restoration of the external fabric of St Mary's Church. The entire structure was re-faced in knapped flint with ashlar stone dressings. The tower was also rebuilt with a new clock and the octagonal staircase was topped with a prominent spirelet.

All Saints' Church, Coleshill

The spirit of reform in the Church of England in the 19th century led to the building of many new churches, as well as the restoration of old ones. As early as 1650, a Parliamentary survey of livings had found that the whole of the parish of Amersham produced tithes to the value of £300. Of this sum £50 was contributed by the 400 inhabitants of the hamlet of Coleshill. The surveyors stated that a 'church were fit to be erected, and endowed with the tithes thereof, the people earnestly desiring the same'.[15] The residents of Coleshill continued to attend St Mary's Church, Amersham until in 1860 a new church was built to serve the hamlet. It was constructed of brick and flint, and had a weather-boarded bell turret. It was designed by George Street, the architect of the Diocese of Oxford. He built six other new churches in the county and restored about forty others.

99 The non-denominational Free Church, on Sycamore Road, was built in 1911. It was replaced by the present building in Woodside Road in 1962.

St George's Church, Amersham Common

The first church in Amersham on the Hill was a mission church, run by the curate from St Mary's. Services were held in the new school on White Lion Road. In 1907, a former contractor's hut, made of corrugated iron and brick, was erected to the west of the school. This served as St Mary's Mission Church until 1935, when the present St George's Church was erected. The new site was further along White Lion Road, where the new church could serve the growing community of Little Chalfont.

St Michael's Church, Amersham on the Hill

As the commercial and social centre of Amersham on the Hill grew up along Hill Avenue and Sycamore Road, St Mary's Mission Church on White Lion Road must have seemed a little remote. St Michael's Mission Church was therefore established in 1920, next to the Free Church, on Sycamore Road. This temporary building was set back from the road and was designed to become a church hall as soon as a new church could be built. With no sign of a permanent building, another

church hall was built in front of the Mission Church in 1927. In fact these two temporary buildings survived until the 1960s and it wasn't until 1966 that a purpose-built St Michael's Church was opened.

The Free Church, Amersham on the Hill

The Free Church at Amersham on the Hill was very much the brainchild of Alfred Ellis, a prominent London solicitor and supporter of the Baptist cause, who came to Amersham on the Hill in 1906. He lived at Fulbeck, The Avenue, and soon began holding meetings at nearby Turret House. In 1911, a site on Sycamore Road was acquired, and the Free Church was erected to the designs of Ellis's friend and business associate, John Harold Kennard.[16] Another supporter of the Free Church was William Lemming, a partner with Alfred Ellis in several early property developments in Amersham on the Hill and Chesham Bois. The old Free Church served well until 1962 when it was replaced by the present building on Woodside Road. The old building was demolished in April 1963.

Eight

Schools

Prior to the English Reformation, the wealthy were able to make bequests to local hospitals and chantries in the knowledge that the clerics in charge would not only pray for their immortal souls, but also apply some of the income from these bequests to the maintenance and education of the poor. After the dissolution of the monasteries, the corporations of Buckingham and Wycombe managed to persuade the Crown not to appropriate all the income of the hospitals and chantries in their towns, but to use some of the funds to establish grammar schools.

There is no evidence that the priest employed by Amersham's Fraternity of St Katherine educated the members' children, so it may be pure coincidence that a school was set up in the Fraternity building, later known as the Church House, 80 years after the suppression of the chantries.

Dr. Challoner's Grammar School
It was not until the 1620s that the rector, Robert Challoner, and the squire, William Tothill of Shardeloes, made some provision for the education

100   The Grammar School founded under the terms of the will of the Rev. Robert Challoner occupied this building in front of the parish church until 1905.

101 Amersham's National School was built on Back Lane in 1873. It was designed for 284 pupils. It has been known as St Mary's School since 1891.

of the poor. Challoner was lucky enough to occupy one of the wealthiest rectories in the country. In his will, made in June 1620, he left to his trustees the rent from a farm in Wavendon, in north Buckinghamshire,

> to erect a free Grammar School in Amersham in the County of Bucks, to be established by deed of feoffment or otherwise as their wisdoms can devise, the town and parish allotting their churchhouse for the schoolhouse, or my successor a tenement in the occupation of Enoch Wyer, now or late, for the dwellinghouse of the Schoolmaster, whom I will to be chosen by my executors, my successor and Mr Tothill, and afterwards by my successors and six of the eldest feoffees and cheifest … Orders for the school I desire my successor to procure from the best ordered school.

Robert Challoner died in 1624 and the school was established in the Church House, with the curate of the parish doubling up as schoolmaster. The foundation date is fixed in local memory by the suspiciously modern inscription on the lintel over the door to the building, which was inserted in the 19th century.

Robert Challoner was not to know that, within twenty years of his own death, the country would be plunged into civil war and that his successor

would be forced to resign from the rectory of Amersham. It is small wonder that even after the Restoration, the Amersham churchwardens should complain to the Bishop of Lincoln in 1662, that 'We have a free grammar school founded by Dr Challoner, late Rector the Church of Amersham, and £20 per annum for ever by decree in Chancery and is no way ordered or governed as it ought to be nor the revenues thereof employed according to the intentions of the founder, nor of such grants and ordinances as have been made concerning the same.'[1]

Cheyne's Writing School

Perhaps Robert Challoner had overestimated the demand in a small market town for a traditional grammar school. The children of the better-off farmers and tradesmen needed first to read and write before they could learn Latin and Greek. Whilst only a handful of boys attended the grammar school, much larger numbers went to Cheyne's Writing School. This more practical education was provided in 1698 by another benefactor, William Lord Cheyne, lord of the manor of Chesham Bois, who set aside £20 per annum, charged on land in Amersham, to employ a schoolmaster to teach writing and arithmetic. For many years, the Writing School

102 A group of teachers at St Mary's School, about 1900.

was accommodated in the Church House, alongside the Grammar School. By 1867, however, it had expanded greatly, with 80 girls at the Church House and 76 boys being taught at the Market Hall.[2]

The British School

Both the Grammar School and the Writing School were closely linked to the Church of England and therefore held no attraction for parents from the strong nonconformist community in Amersham. In 1842, a British School was established at the Baptist Lower Meeting House. It received a grant from the British and Foreign School Society, promoters of non-denominational education. British schools were characterised by the employment of older pupils to teach the younger ones, and by the pupils moving backwards and forwards in the rows of desks, according to their academic success.

The National Schools

The promoters of the 1870 Education Act sought to ensure that every child would receive an elementary education. This was to be provided either by voluntary effort, or by the establishment of a school board supported by a local school rate. The nonconformists preferred the school board option as it would be free from control by the rector, but the threat of a school rate persuaded the majority to go along with the voluntary principle. A committee was formed in 1872 to receive subscriptions towards building a new National School, that is one supported by the National Society for the Education of the Poor in the Principles of the Established Church. The committee, dominated by the Drake and Weller families, raised £1,350 to build National schools at Amersham and Woodrow. The rector,

103 The new Grammar School at Amersham on the Hill was built in 1905, in the fashionable Arts and Crafts style, to the designs of H. Belch.

104 The London architects, Kemp & How, designed further Arts and Crafts style buildings at Dr. Challoner's Grammar School in 1910.

105   The county architect, Fred Pooley, took responsibility for the late 1950s buildings at Dr. Challoner's Grammar School.

Edward Tyrwhitt-Drake, provided a site on Back Lane for a school for 284 pupils, whilst the squire, Thomas Tyrwhitt-Drake, gave a site at Woodrow for a school for 30 children. The two schools opened in September 1873.   Woodrow school was closed in 1905 and converted into a private house in 1912.[3] The National School at Coleshill had been built in 1847 on land provided by Lord Curzon. By 1891 it was attracting an average attendance of 73 children. A small school was erected in 1869 on Raans Road, Amersham Common. This was replaced in 1901 by a larger school on White Lion Road, now known as St George's School. The earlier building became a lodge to George Weller's house, The Plantation, and survives as a private house today.

The New Grammar School

The 1902 Education Act gave Buckinghamshire County Council control of elementary and secondary education across the county. The former church schools were in fact little changed, but the grammar schools were all given larger premises and scholarships were provided for those who could pass an entrance examination. In 1905, Dr. Challoner's Grammar School moved to new premises at Amersham on the Hill, on a site provided by William Wykeham Tyrwhitt-Drake. The original architect was H. Belch, but the highly respected firm of Kemp & How put up the later buildings in the Arts and Crafts style.[4] For the first time, girls were admitted to the school, which had places for 90 children.

Following the 1944 Education Act, which provided secondary education for all, Dr. Challoner's Grammar School was designated as the local grammar school. It remained co-educational until 1962, when a new grammar school for girls was built at Cokes Lane. Initially, Amersham's secondary modern pupils went to Germains Schools and White Hill Schools in Chesham. The need to travel to Chesham was partly eliminated in 1956 when a co-educational secondary modern school was built in Raans Road. This became boys only when Brudenell Secondary Modern School was built on Stanley Hill in 1967. The two secondary modern schools later joined on the Stanley Hill site as the Amersham School.

Nine

Caring for the Poor

The dissolution of the monasteries under Henry VIII removed the only institutions which had any responsibility for the care of the nation's poor. Under Edward VI, chantries were also dissolved, including Amersham's Fraternity of St Katherine, which had carried out various civic and charitable duties as well as maintaining a chantry chapel in the church. Its work may have continued on a voluntary basis, and no doubt the town took advantage of an Act of

Parliament of 1572 which enabled parishes to appoint officials to collect donations for the poor. These officials became known as overseers of the poor. An Act of 1597 empowered them to levy poor rates and, in 1601, further legislation enabled them to build parish workhouses.

It is clear from the Amersham overseers accounts of 1617 that part of the former Fraternity House by the churchyard, now called the Church House,

106 This house in the High Street was left by William Tothill in 1626 as a linen factory where the poor of Amersham might be found work. It remained in operation until 1789. The photograph shows the building decorated for the coronation of Edward VII in 1901.

107   A workhouse was opened in 1726 to accommodate poor people who could not be maintained in their own houses. It was built next to the Grammar School, between the churchyard and these cottages, which stood in the middle of the Broadway.

was not only a venue for town meetings, but was also being used 'to set the poor to work in linen'.[1] Spinning wheels, hand cards and looms were provided, and John Gregory was appointed to supervise the work. Even though Amersham's Church House was hardly adequate for these functions, it was required in 1624 to house the grammar school founded by the trustees of the late rector, Dr. Robert Challoner.

Tothill's Workhouse

William Tothill, of Shardeloes, was evidently aware of these problems. In his will, proved in London in 1627, he bequeathed a house in the High Street (now called Frith House) to be run as a linen manufactory, where the poor of Amersham could find gainful employment. He provided an endowment of £500 with which his trustees purchased a 47-acre farm in Chesham. The rent

from this property was to pay the governor of the workhouse a salary, to keep the workhouse in repair and to provide machinery and a stock of linen which the poor could turn into saleable products. One of the early governors of the workhouse was a linen weaver named William Rutt, who built up the stock of the workhouse to a value of £170. His widow, Elizabeth Rutt, continued the workhouse until 1696, when Montague Drake appointed Gyles Child as governor. Gyles Child and his assistant, James Norwood, mismanaged the workhouse so badly that an enquiry was held into the running of the charity in 1701.[2] Another enquiry in 1746 found fault with the then governor, John Jennings.[3] Successive governors seemed to employ fewer poor people than the trustees hoped, failed to pay them the minimum wages laid down in the rules of the charity, and ran down the stock of materials in the workhouse. By 1789, the workhouse was disused

108   About 1780, the workhouse inmates were moved to a larger building in Whielden Street. The building later became Fuller's drapery store.

and the house on the High Street was let to William Morten, a wealthy lace dealer. The charity's original objects were met by renting a house on the High Street, next to the path to the Baptist Meeting House, in which a hemp-dresser named Richard Hodgkinson employed some of the poor to manufacture sacks. Others were employed at the cotton mill near the Bury Mill, built by the Baptist minister, Richard Morris. By 1828, William Tothill's Trustees applied all the income of the charity to the placement of poor children as apprentices.[4]

The Parish Workhouse

William Tothill's workhouse had been intended to provide a space in which the poor could be put to work, rather than a place where the homeless might live. The overseers still had to pay part or all of the rents of some poor families to enable them to stay in their own homes. This was considered by many to encourage idleness, so, under a new Act of Parliament in 1722, overseers of the poor were encouraged to build or rent workhouses in which the poor could be accommodated together. This was likely to be less attractive to claimants and would be a safety net for the truly destitute. The Act enabled overseers of the poor to contract out the running of their workhouses to suitable local businessmen. At a meeting in Amersham in 1724, it was decided to erect a new workhouse to the east of the Church House.[5] A local carpenter, named Stephen Squier, completed the new building in 1726, at a cost of £160. The poor were required

109 Amersham Union Workhouse was built to house the poor of Amersham and several surrounding parishes including Chesham. It was designed in 1838 by the famous church architect, George Gilbert Scott.

to work to offset the cost of their maintenance and in 1741, the overseers raised £57 by the sale of woollen yarn spun by the inmates. This workhouse is shown on the 1742 map of the Borough of Amersham. It continued in use until about 1780, when the poor were moved to a much larger building around the corner, now numbered 20-28 Whielden Street. In 1798, the governor of this workhouse was William Andrew. In the 1830 directory, Daniel Smith is listed as the governor of the workhouse.

The Union Workhouse

Under the Poor Law Amendment Act of 1834, separate provision for the poor of each parish was replaced with a system where up to twenty or more parishes formed a Union and concentrated their resources in one workhouse, sited in the largest town in the area. Each Union was to be run by a board of guardians, who could raise poor rates across the Union to pay for the scheme. Amersham was chosen as the centre for such a Union, much to the disgust of neighbouring Chesham, which had a larger population. The Union included Beaconsfield, Chalfont St Peter, Chalfont St Giles, Chenies, Chesham, Chesham Bois, Coleshill, Great Missenden, the Lee, Penn and Seer Green. Because a union workhouse could not be planned and built overnight, it was decided to house all male paupers at the existing Amersham parish workhouse, all the women at Chesham and all the children at Chenies. On 23 May 1835, an angry mob disrupted the first

110   William Drake's Almshouses were built in 1657 for six poor widows over the age of fifty.

attempt to transfer the male paupers from Chesham to Amersham, but the division of the sexes was carried through. In 1838, the Buckinghamshire architect, George Gilbert Scott, was appointed to design a new Union Workhouse to be sited on the southern extremity of the town. It was ready to receive the first inmates on 29 September 1839.[6] The old workhouse on Whielden Street reverted to the Drake family and was divided into several tenements. The most prominent was that of Henry Fuller, a draper and outfitter who occupied what is now 28 Whielden Street. He bought the premises at the 1928 sale of Drake property in the town.

By 1930, the infirmaries attached to workhouses were becoming as important as the accommodation they provided for older and destitute people. A new Act of Parliament transferred control of work-houses from boards of guardians to local authorities. Amersham Union Workhouse became a Public

Assistance Institution run by Buckinghamshire County Council. In 1939, an Emergency Services Hospital, serving the local civilian and military population, was added to Public Assistance Institution. Huts were erected to the south of the 1838 workhouse building. The creation of the National Health Service in 1948 saw the Public Assistance Institution and Emergency Services Hospital combined as Amersham General Hospital, part of Oxford Regional Hospital Board.

Almshouses

It was fashionable in the 17th and 18th centuries for gentlemen and successful tradesmen to build almshouses for the more deserving poor of their native towns. There were three such foundations in Amersham and two remain in existence today. The best known of the almshouses are those built by William Drake in 1657. When William Drake

111 The four single-storey cottages on the north side of the High Street were almshouses provided by Andrew Hall, of Amersham, who died in 1697.

died in 1669, the almshouses were occupied by six poor widows over the age of 50, one of whom, Ann Child, acted as warden. The women each received a new gown every two years, which they were to wear every Sunday, when attending the parish church. They also received an allowance of 2s. each Saturday and free firewood for their hearths. In his will, made in 1667 but proved in 1669, William Drake nominated governors of the Almshouses and left Burtons Farm, Chalfont St Giles,

extending to 183 acres, as an endowment. His executors accepted that the rent from Burtons Farm was insufficient to pay the expenses of the Almshouses, so they created an £11 annual rent charge, payable to the governors of the Almshouses, out of Stockings Farm in Coleshill. The income of the Almshouses was further increased by a bequest of £300 in the will of William Drake, who died in 1796. In 1851, the Drake almshouses were occupied by Maria Ebbs, aged 57, widow of a

112 The entry to the left of the post office originally led to a row of cottages known as Hatch's Yard. These were demolished in 1875 and replaced by a row of almshouses endowed by Harriett Day. The photograph shows the post office decorated for Queen Victoria's Diamond Jubilee in 1897.

113 Harriett Day's Almshouses, viewed from the meadow across the River Misbourne, in 1992.

labourer; Ellen Priest, aged 80, late postmistress; Mary Tapping, aged 75, widow of a sack carrier; Mary Chapman, aged 78, daughter of a tailor; Sarah Butcher, aged 74, formerly a baker; and Alice Barker, aged 71, a chair woman. In 1925, the inmates each received 7s. per week.

Until the building of the Methodist church on the site in 1899, four single-storey cottages stood opposite the *Swan Inn*. These belonged to the trustees of Andrew Hall of Amersham, yeoman, who lived near Little Shardeloes on the site of the present Hinton House, and died in 1697. It was his intention that his trustees and the churchwardens of Amersham should select some poor aged men or women, being single and without children, to live in the cottages for life or for so long a time as the trustees should think fit. The Charity Commissioners, reporting on Hall's Charity in 1833, stated that 'the buildings are at present time converted into four cottages, which are occupied rent free by four poor widows, constant attenders at church'.[7] In 1851, the houses were occupied by Dorcas Turner, aged 51, a pillow lace maker; Sarah

Hailey, aged 77, a pauper; Dennis Brown, aged 62, a pauper; and Elizabeth Saunders, aged 80, also a pauper. Although three of the cottages were still occupied in 1891, their condition was so poor that they were demolished and the site sold to the Methodists in 1899.

The third block of almshouses was built as late as 1875 by Harriett Day, whose family had kept the *Swan Inn* for many years. Until her death in 1880, she had lived with her brother, William Day, at the house once called Liscar, but now known as Hinton House. The almshouses were built on the site of a row of poor cottages in the Franchise of Amersham called Hatch's Yard, which had been occupied by labourers and chair makers. In 1881, the new almshouses were occupied by Hannah Woodbridge, Mary Ann Glenister, Ann Wilkins, Mary Penn, Eleanor Cox and Rose Turner. A report of 1925 described the trust estate as six freehold cottages in an alley at the rear of the Post Office. The endowment produced £90 per year, of which the inmates received 7s. a week.[8]

Ten

The Railway and Amersham on the Hill

The history of Amersham might have been very different had the London to Birmingham Railway adopted George Stephenson's preferred route along the Misbourne valley. Local opposition, particularly from the Drake family, contributed to the decision to route the line through the Tring, rather than the Wendover gap.[1] It was to be a further fifty years before Amersham was connected to the railway network, years during which the nation's population doubled, whilst Amersham's population declined by 10 per cent. The London to Birmingham Railway, later known as the London and North Western Railway, opened in 1838, its tracks skirting the east side of Buckinghamshire. Branches were built to Aylesbury in 1839 and Buckingham in 1850. The Great Western line to Bristol, also opened in 1838, cut across the south of the county, with a branch to High Wycombe opened in 1854 and an extension to Aylesbury opened in 1863. Amersham was left in the no-man's-land in between, with neither the L & NWR nor the GWR seeing any merit in building a line to a small market town with a population of only three thousand. Those in Amersham needing to conduct business in the capital still had to board the old-fashioned stage-coach which ran from Wendover to London, or take the 2½-hour journey by railway coach from the *Griffin Inn* to meet the trains at Watford station.

The Metropolitan Railway

Amersham might never have had a railway, but for the ambition of Edward Watkin, chairman of the Manchester, Sheffield and Lincolnshire Railway (later to become the Great Central Railway). In 1872, he was appointed chairman of the Metropolitan Railway and saw a line along the Misbourne valley towards Aylesbury as a possible through route from London to Manchester. He soon developed an understanding with the 2nd Duke of Buckingham, who, as chairman of the recently opened Aylesbury to Buckingham Railway, had in 1871 secured an Act of Parliament for an Aylesbury to London Railway. This would have linked Aylesbury, via Amersham, to the LNWR branch line from Watford to Rickmansworth. Watkin persuaded the Aylesbury and Buckingham to seek further powers to extend their proposed line south from Rickmansworth to meet a new Metropolitan Railway extension to Harrow. Each company secured Parliamentary approval for their schemes in 1874, enabling the two chairmen to stake a claim to the route, whilst they endeavoured to raise sufficient funds to build the lines. Although nothing came of the Aylesbury to Rickmansworth scheme, the Metropolitan Railway opened their line to Harrow in 1880, and secured an Act of Parliament for its further extension to Rickmansworth.[2]

Chesham gets its Railway first

In 1881, the Metropolitan Railway introduced a Bill into Parliament to create a Rickmansworth to Aylesbury Railway Company, but the L & NWR opposed the scheme and introduced a rival Bill to extend their Rickmansworth branch along a similar route to Chesham. With twice the population of Amersham, Chesham had a greater potential to contribute revenue to either of these railway companies. Although it was the Aylesbury and Rickmansworth Railway Bill which was passed, Sir Edward Watkin, still open to any proposal which would bring his MS & LR trains into London, maintained a dialogue with the L & NWR about a joint line, leaving the London

114   A Metropolitan Railway train at Amersham Station in 1935.

115   A London & North Eastern Railway train at Amersham Station.

116   Station Road was built to link the new Metropolitan Railway station with the old town in the 1890s.

to Birmingham main line at Tring and going through Chesham to Rickmansworth. Even though the L & NWR eventually dropped their plans for a joint line, the Metropolitan Railway pressed on, opening their line from Harrow to Rickmansworth in 1887 and from there to Chesham in 1889. The Metropolitan line to Chesham followed the ridge between the Misbourne and Chess valleys as far as Amersham Common, before swinging north towards Chesham. The nearest station to Amersham was built just within Chalfont St Giles parish and was therefore called Chalfont Road Station. A horse-drawn omnibus from the *Griffin Hotel* in Amersham met each train, but took 35 minutes to reach the town.

The Metropolitan Railway now turned its attention back towards the Misbourne valley and in 1887 began buying land for an extension to Aylesbury. The Drake family no longer opposed

the scheme, and readily agreed to sell the necessary land from Weedon Hill and Hyrons Farms. Other land in Amersham came from George Weller, owner of Woodside Farm and The Plantation, and from Lord Chesham, who owned Raans Farm in Amersham parish and Loudhams Farm in neighbouring Chalfont St Giles. The Metropolitan Railway completed negotiations for the purchase of the Aylesbury and Buckingham Railway in 1889 and opened the extension from Chalfont Road to Aylesbury in 1892. Chalfont Road Station now became a junction and the line to Chesham one of the shortest branches in the country.

Amersham Station
Amersham Station was opened in September 1892. It was sited two-thirds of a mile north of the town on land formerly belonging to the rectory.

117 The stylish Edwardian house at Beech Grove, off station Road, was built about 1910. It is now numbered 65 Station Road.

118 The *Station Hotel* was built in 1893 by Weller & Co.

119   Another new road was laid out from the railway station to join Chesham Road. It became known as Hill Avenue and at first contained more private houses than shops.

The old road from Amersham up Rectory Hill was thought too steep for an access road, so Station Road, a more gradual climb from the Bury End of the old town, was laid out by the Metropolitan Railway Company. The brewer George Weller was one of the first of the locals to appreciate the opportunity for development that the railway afforded. In 1893, he built the *Station Hotel* opposite the railway station, closing the *Black Horse* and transferring the licence to the new hotel. He also laid out building plots on that part of Station Road which passed through his Woodside Farm.

The Development of Amersham on the Hill

The Cavendishes of Latimer House, owners of Raans Farm, were also aware of the increased value of their land on Amersham Common. In 1894 they laid out building plots between the railway and the north side of White Lion Road, all the way from the former *Black Horse Inn* to Chalfont Road Station. The Duke of Bedford was appalled and secured all the lots for £13,000 to prevent development near to his Chenies Estate. By 1920, the Duke of Bedford's attitude had changed. He sold the land for building, including the farmland on which the village of Little Chalfont was

120 An aerial view of Amersham on the Hill, taken in 1920, shows Elm Close under construction, just north of the railway station.

subsequently built.[3] The Drake family of Shardeloes, once vehement opponents of a railway through the Misbourne valley, were happy to exploit their property near the new station. Their estate agents pegged out new roads over the northern fields of Hyrons Farm and laid out hundreds of building plots, comprising Longfield Drive, Hervines Road, Devonshire Avenue and Parkfield Avenue.[4] It was to be many years before all these roads were lined with new houses, but successive sales of building land enabled the Drake family to maintain their position as one of the leading county families until the outbreak of the Second World War.

The idea of escaping from London to the leafy suburbs was popularised by such publications as *Where Shall We Live?*, which described each home counties town and listed the new housing estates then under construction. The 1908 edition carried an advertisement for a new development planned by J.W. Falkner & Sons, of Old Kent Road, London, who had purchased the land on which Hill Avenue was later built.

Amersham Hill Estate, adjoining Amersham Station of the Great Central and Metropolitan Railways and only 35 minutes journey from London. A high, dry and bracing situation in a beautiful district close to the Common. The estate will be laid out in the latest and most approved principles and the houses will be artistically designed under the direct supervision of a well known London architect with the additional advantage of being thoroughly well built. Freehold land, shops and houses to be let or sold. For particulars apply to Messrs J.W. Falkner & Sons on the estate, or to Percy A. Hopkins, The Old Grammar School, Amersham.

The project was evidently not a success, for development was very slow, and in 1920 Alfred Falkner sold a large part of the estate to the Amersham Public Utility Society for the construction of Elm Close.

Builders

Local builders were also quick to spot opportunities for profit. Prominent amongst the builders was Alfred Woodley, who was born in Chesham in

121 These semi-detached houses on Stanley Hill were built by Robin Brazil in 1932.

122 Normandy, Devonshire Avenue, was built for Charles Wood in 1926.

123 Old Timbers, Devonshire Avenue, was built for Edward Parker in 1927.

1876. He bought several plots of land when the former Bent's Charity land, adjacent to Chesham Bois Common, was sold in 1908. He lived at Longwood, on South Road, near to his builder's yard in Lexham Gardens. He later built many private houses for clients and became a large private landlord, renting out houses in Highland Road, The Meadows and Quarrenden Road. A prominent liberal, he became a district and county councillor and member of the board of guardians. He was also chairman of Amersham Football Club.

Another prominent builder was William Collins Matthews, who was born in Chesham Bois in 1884, the son of an artist named James Matthews. With his brother, James D. Matthews, he began to build houses in Amersham on the Hill about

124 High and Over was designed by Amyas Connell, in the style of Le Corbusier, in 1929.

125 The Sun Houses, also designed by Amyas Connell, were built on the drive to High and Over in 1935.

126   This row of shops on Station Road was built in 1907 and styled 'Station Parade'.

1910. They built several large houses in Weedon Lane in 1926. In the same year they put up the extravagantly half-timbered 'Normandy' in Devonshire Avenue for Charles Wood, the owner of a chain of London grocery stores. In 1927 they built the neighbouring 'Old Timbers' for Edward Parker, a director of the Army and Navy Stores. William Matthews lived at Thornview, Chestnut Lane. He died there in 1933. Other well-known builders were Robin Brazil, Station Road; George Darlington, High Street, Amersham; Ernest J. Gee, High Street, Chesham; William Gomme,

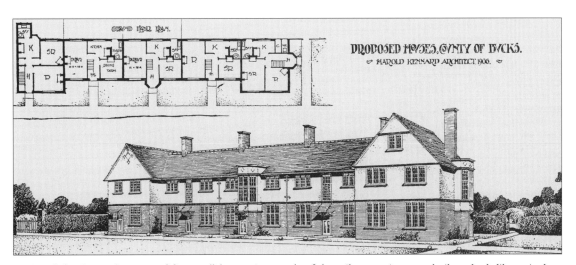

127   'The Avenue', a row of five small houses just south of the railway station, was built to look like a single country house. It was designed by John Harold Kennard in 1906.

128 Hervines Road, off Chesham Road, became a very fashionable address. 'The Gables' was designed by John Harold Kennard in 1910.

129 This pair of semi-detached houses on South Road were designed by John Harold Kennard in 1907.

130   Building construction at Elm Close, 1920.

Copperkins Lane, Chesham Bois; George Pearce;
Rust & Ratcliffe, Higham Road, Chesham; Arthur
Saunders, Woodside Road; and Fred P. Williams,
Nazing Cottage, Station Road.

Architects
Although many of the smaller houses were designed
and erected by local builders, some of the larger
villas and small country houses were individually
designed by leading London architects such as Kemp
& How and Forbes & Tate. In 1929, Bernard
Ashmole, at that time Professor of Archaeology at
London University, employed the architect Amyas
Connell to build a country house off Station Road
in the style of Le Corbusier. 'High and Over' was
perhaps the first house in England in this style.
Connell also designed the 'Sun Houses' which line
the drive to High and Over.

John Harold Kennard, with offices in Grays
Inn Road, London and in Amersham, was not a
famous architect, but he made a far greater
contribution to the local landscape than any other
builder or architect. He was born in 1883, the
son of John Moir Kennard, an architect in
Bermondsey, South London. About 1906, he
formed a partnership with an Amersham architect
and entrepreneur called William Sumner, who
worked from the offices on Station Road now
occupied by Amersham Town Council. This firm
built the row of shops by the railway bridge called
Station Parade and the nearby shop and house
called Turret House. In 1906, John Kennard
designed the terrace of five elegant houses on the
Avenue, off Station Road.[5] Kennard also designed
several large houses on Hervines Road, including
'The Gables', built in 1910.[6]

131 The new houses at Elm Close, 1920.

132 John Harold Kennard's plan for a pair of semi-detached houses in Elm Close, 1920.

John Harold Kennard became an ARIBA in 1910, by which time he had moved to Chesham Bois. He was associated with John William Falkner & Sons, the developers of Hill Avenue. He was also linked in some way to William Lemming, the developer of the Oakfield Estate. He was probably a director of other property development companies active in Amersham on the Hill, such as the Chesham Bois Development Company and Rural Homes Ltd. About 1910, he designed three similar chalet-style houses, two at Beech Grove, off Station Road, and another on Chesham Road, opposite the entrance to Hervines Road.

In 1911, John Kennard designed the new Free Church on Sycamore Road for his friend Alfred Ellis. Perhaps his most interesting experiment was in 1920, when he built 30 semi-detached houses on Elm Close for the Amersham Public Utility

133 This 'cottage' on Chesham Road, is typical of the small country houses designed by John Harold Kennard around 1910.

134 John Harold Kennard designed the striking row of shops on the corner of Chesham Road and Sycamore Road in 1912. The centre shop was first occupied by his brother, Arthur Moir Kennard, a chemist.

135 John Harold Kennard also designed the next row of shops along Chesham Road, built in 1913.

136 John Harold Kennard designed most of the houses in Bois Avenue. He himself lived in a smaller house in Chiltern Avenue.

137   Pretty & Ellis, originally based in Great Missenden, were one of the first firms of estate agents to open an office in Amersham on the Hill.

Society. This was another development company with Kennard as the architect, Alfred Ellis as the solicitor, and Harvey Ellis and Charles Alderson, of Pretty, Ellis & Alderson, as estate agents. The houses were built with a grant under the 1919 Housing and Town Planning Act, which gave the Ministry of Health powers to assist local housing projects with state subsidies. Due to shortages of materials, the houses were constructed out of concrete blocks cast on site. The first floors were made of rein-forced concrete, the windows of stove enamelled steel, and the window sills of tile, thus eliminating the need for complex joinery.[7] The same syndicate submitted a plan to erect a similar estate of subsi-dised houses in Chesham Bois, styling themselves the Chesham Bois Public Utility Society, but the scheme was dropped.

In 1912, John Kennard designed one of the major landmarks of Amersham on the Hill, the block of five shops and houses in mock-Tudor style at Oakfield Corner. His brother, Arthur Kennard, opened a pharmacy in the prominent corner shop. In 1913, he designed a further block of four shops on Chesham Road and a similar block of five shops on Sycamore Road. John Kennard went on to design at least one quarter of the Arts and Crafts style houses built in Amersham on the Hill and Chesham Bois before the Great War. He built most of the houses in Bois Avenue and, of course, designed his own home, 'Rosemarie', Chiltern Avenue. This small semi-bungalow still stands, although it is now called 'Blackdown'. In 1921, John Kennard moved to a new house in Hervines Road. He died there in 1926 at the early age of 42.[8]

Solicitors
Local solicitors not only profited from the legal fees involved in conveying so many new properties,

138 F.E. Howard & Son opened these offices on the corner of Sycamore Road about 1920.

but also dealt in land themselves. Clement Cheese's name often appears in the lists of new developments passed by the Amersham Rural District Council. He lived at the palatial Elmodesham House in the old town. Alfred Ellis was a prominent London solicitor who came to Amersham about 1906. He numbered amongst his clients the National Farmers Union and the Baptist Union of Great Britain and Ireland. He was one of the directors of Rural Homes Ltd., which, in 1915, built The Woodlands, a terrace of six houses, designed by John Kennard, which runs down the hill from Long Park Road, Chesham Bois. Alfred Ellis also acted for the Amersham Public Utility Society. He was a prime mover in the building of the Free Church in 1911, and was a prominent local preacher. He lived at Fulbeck, The Avenue, where he died in 1936, aged 68.[9]

Estate Agents

Several estate agents were heavily involved in the development of Amersham on the Hill. The firm of Pretty, Ellis and Alderson comprised Edwin Pretty, an estate agent and insurance broker from Great Missenden, J.W. Harvey Ellis of The Hollies, Grimsdell's Lane, and Charles H. Alderson of Sycamore Road. Both Ellis and Alderson were directors of the Amersham Public Utility Society. Pretty & Ellis had a temporary wooden office outside the railway station, but later moved to the corner of Hill Avenue and Elm Close. Francis Edward Howard was a Chesham estate agent who took his son, Charles Ewart Howard, into partnership and opened offices on the corner of Hill Avenue and Sycamore Road about 1920. He was the first chairman of the Amersham Public Utility Society.

139 Sycamore Road was at first a residential area. Sainsbury's needed to demolish two relatively new houses to build the parade of shops on the west side of the road.

140 The Regent Cinema was built on Sycamore Road in 1928.

141   Sycamore Road about 1950, with the Free Church and St Michael's Church on the left.

Although Pretty & Ellis and F.E. Howard & Son styled themselves as architects and surveyors, the firm of Swannell & Sly were by far the most active of the estate agents in actually designing new houses. From his base in the High Street, Rickmansworth, William Henry Swannell extended his business to include offices in Pinner, Northwood, Moor Park, Rickmansworth, Chorley Wood, Little Chalfont, Amersham, Great Missenden and Wendover. The Amersham office, at the bottom of Hill Avenue, was established about 1910. By 1930 the partners were J.T. Sly, A.E. Parkes and Alec T.

Sly. In conjunction with the builder, William Matthews, Swannell & Sly designed many of the houses on Devonshire Avenue, Copperkins Lane and Weedon Lane.

Amersham Rural District Council also contributed to the growth of Amersham on the Hill by erecting several estates of council houses. Some of the first were at Stanley Hill where 30 houses were built in 1920. They were designed by the leading architects, Kemp & How. More houses were built at the corner of Bell Lane and White Lion Road, on a plot of land purchased at the

142 Semi-detached houses at Woodside Close, built by the Metropolitan Railway Country Estates Ltd. in 1930. Further 'Metroland' houses were built at Highfield Close, The Drive and Batchelors Way.

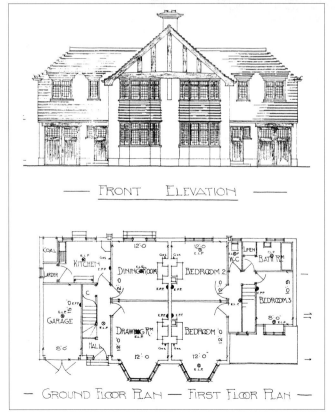

— FRONT ELEVATION —

— GROUND FLOOR PLAN — FIRST FLOOR PLAN —

143 The architect's drawing for typical 'Metro-land' houses at Woodside Close, 1930.

auction of outlying parts of the Chenies Estate in 1920. In the 1930s, the Rural District Council built more council houses at New Road, Plantation Way and Weller Road, all on parts of Hyrons Farm sold by the Drake family.

One notable developer was Sainsbury's. The firm purchased two relatively new houses on Sycamore Road and replaced them with the handsome row of nine shops named Chiltern Parade, completed in 1937. The tenants included such household names as Boots the Chemists and Freeman, Hardy & Willis. The three-storey block, in Georgian style, contrasted strongly with the mock-Tudor of the earlier 'Metro-land' shops on Sycamore Road. There were nine flats above the shops, each with three elegant sash windows on the first and second floors.

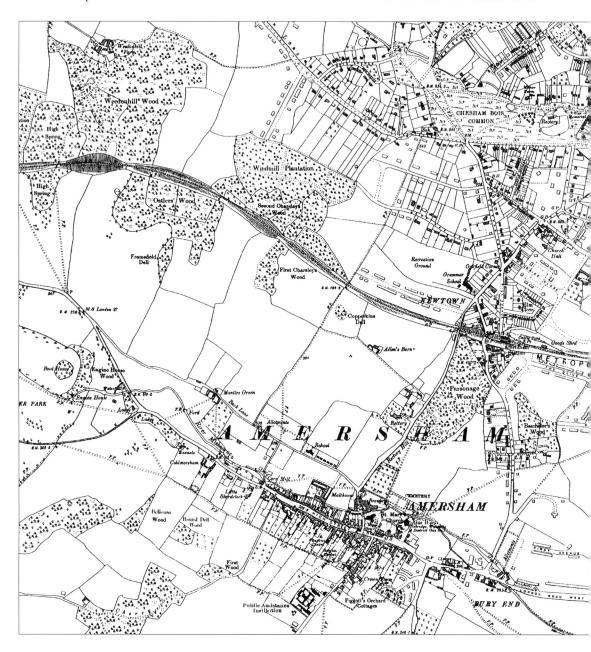

Metropolitan Railway Country Estates Ltd.

The firm which did most to give Amersham on the Hill a uniform style was the Metropolitan Railway Country Estates Ltd. The company purchased Woodside Farm from the executors of George Weller in 1930. Their new houses, designed by W.H. Dungworth, were advertised in their own publication, *Metro-land*, in 1932.

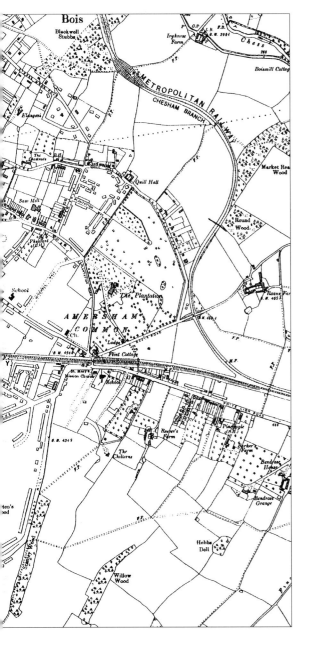

The Weller Estate, Amersham. 500 feet above sea level and adjacent to Amersham Station, with excellent service of trains to and from Baker Street and City Stations. This beautifully situated estate of 78 acres adjoins Amersham Station on both sides of the railway. The southern part of the estate embraces Batchelor's Wood, where some exceptional sites fronting Station Road and overlooking old Amersham and fine stretches of country, can now be obtained for immediate building. Ready-made frontage to public and new roads is also available, and excellent shop sites can be obtained. Included in the estate north of the line is Woodside Farm, built in 1670 by Mary Pennington and associated with Cromwell, Penn and the Quakers. This is for sale freehold. A few semi-detached and detached houses with built in garages are now available at £875 to £1225 freehold with no road charges and no stamp duties. Total deposit £25. Full particulars and a plan of the estate may be obtained on application to: H. Gibson, The Metropolitan Railway Country Estates, Ltd. General Offices: Baker Street Station, N.W.1.

In 1948, Amersham Rural District Council purchased Woodside Farm and 18 acres of land not yet built upon as a site for a Civic Centre. The project was delayed for many years, but in 1956 the barns and stables were restored and handed over to Amersham and District Community Association as a Community Centre.[10] The warden, Bernard Colclough, lived in Woodside Farmhouse. The site later accommodated a library (1961), a swimming pool (1966) and a youth centre (1970). The old farmhouse was demolished in the late 1960s. Local government re-organisation in 1974 brought about a forced marriage between Amersham Rural District Council and Chesham Urban District Council to form Chiltern District. The enlarged Council continued to occupy offices at Elmodesham House until 1986 when the original intention of the Rural District Council was achieved, with the completion of the new offices of Chiltern District Council, on land between Woodside Farm and the railway station. Amersham on the Hill thus became the administrative as well as the commercial centre of Amersham.

144 The Ordnance Survey map of 1938 shows the enormous growth of Amersham on the Hill since the opening of the railway in 1892.

Notes

Chapter One

Amersham in Domesday Book, pp.1-7

1. J. Morris (ed.), *Domesday Book, Buckinghamshire* (vol.13, 1978).
2. J. Chenevix Trench, *Rec. Bucks.*, vol.20 (1977), p.412.

Chapter Two

A New Town in the Chilterns, pp.8-14

1. W. Page (ed.), *Victoria History of the County of Buckingham*, vol.3 (1925), p.147.
2. Bucks Record Office Ma/Dr/1t.
3. Page, *Victoria History of the County of Buckingham* vol.3, p.145.
4. Bucks Record Office D/DRD/2/40.
5. L. Toulmin Smith (ed.), *The Itinerary of John Leland* (1964 edition), vol.2, p.113.

Chapter Three

Amersham Farms and Farmers, pp.14-25

1. J. Chenevix Trench, *Rec. Bucks.*, vol.20 (1977), p.414.
2. Bucks Record Office D/DRD/2/22.
3. Bucks Record Office BAS Maps 1.
4. Bucks Record Office D/BASM/2/14.
5. RCHM *Inventory of the Historical Monuments in Buckinghamshire*, vol.1 (1911).
6. I.F.W. Beckett (ed.), *The Buckinghamshire Posse Comitatus 1798* (1985), p.134.
7. J. Chenevix Trench, *Rec. Bucks.*, vol.36 (1994), p.144.

Chapter Four

Trade and Industry, pp.26-46

1. Bucks Record Office D/DRD/2/91.
2. G. Eland, *Rec. Bucks.*, vol.13 (1934), p.361.
3. I.F.W. Beckett (ed.), *The Buckinghamshire Posse Comitatus 1798* (1985), p.173.
4. M. Reed (ed.), *Buckinghamshire Probate Inventories 1661-1714* (1988), p.49.
5. Guildhall Library Mss. 11936/18/35305.
6. Bucks Record Office D/DRD/2/173.
7. Bucks Record Office D/DRD/2/72.
8. Bucks Record Office D/DRD/2/30.
9. G. Eland, *Shardeloes Papers of the 17th and 18th Centuries* (1947), p.27.
10. Bucks Record Office D/BASM/2a/1.
11. Guildhall Library Mss. 11936/258/387733.
12. Bucks Record Office ST/125.
13. Bucks Record Office DX/275/1.
14. B. Godwin, *Memoirs of Richard Morris* (1819).
15. Guildhall Library Mss. 11936/257/382866.
16. A. Morley Davies, *Cambridge County Geographies: Buckinghamshire* (1912), p.98.

Chapter Five

Turnpike Roads and Coaching Inns, pp.47-60

1. Public Record Office WO/30/48.
2. M. Reed (ed.), *Buckinghamshire Probate Inventories 1661-1714* (1988), p.122.
3. Reed (ed.), *Buckinghamshire Probate Inventories*, p.255.
4. Bucks Record Office D/DRD/2/37, 62, 64.
5. R. Gibbs, *History of Aylesbury* (1885), p.576.
6. Bucks Record Office D/DR/12/78.
7. W. Le Hardy (ed.), *Calendar of Quarter Sessions Records, vol.5 1718-1724* (1958), p.73.
8. Bucks Record Office D/DR/5/10.
9. Guildhall Library Mss. 11936/271/408781.
10. K. Edmonds, *Rec. Bucks*, vol.35 (1993), pp.37-9.
11. *Bucks Examiner*, 11 October 1929.
12. G. Eland, *Purefoy Letters 1735-53*, vol.2 (1931), p.361.
13. J.K. Fowler, *Echoes of Old Country Life* (1892), p.213.

14. *Universal British Directory* (1790), p.45.
15. *Pigot and Co.'s Directory* (1830), p.44.

Chapter Six
The Drakes of Shardeloes, pp.61-8
1. G. Eland, *Rec. Bucks.* vol.14 (1941), p.283.
2. Bucks Record Office D/DR/1/1.
3. Bucks Record Office D/DRD/2/35.
4. G. Lipscomb, *History and Antiquities of the County of Buckingham*, vol.3 (1847), p.168.
5. M. Reed (ed.), *Buckinghamshire Probate Inventories 1661-1714* (1988), p.258.
6. R. Sedgwick, *House of Commons 1715-1754*, vol.1 (1970), p.621.
7. Bucks Record Office D/DR/12/61.
8. Bucks Record Office D/DRD/2/123.
9. C.A.M. Press, *Buckinghamshire Leaders, Social and Political* (1905).

Chapter Seven
Churches and Chapels, pp.69-82
1. Bucks Record Office D/DRD/2/35.
2. S.L. Ede-Borrett (ed.), *The Letters of Neremiah Wharton* (1983), p.7.
3. A.G. Matthews, *Calamy Revised* (1934), p.480.
4. Bucks Record Office D/BASM/2a/20.
5. *Calendar of State Papers Domestic, 1653-4*, p.201.
6. C.G. Crump (ed.), *History of the Life of Thomas Ellwood* (1900), p.139.
7. J. Broad (ed.), *Buckinghamshire Dissent and Parish Life 1669-1712* (1993), p.39.
8. J.H. Laverty (ed.), *Amersham Parish Chest*, p.82.
9. Broad (ed.), *Buckinghamshire Dissent and Parish Life*, p.99.
10. E. Legg (ed.), *Buckinghamshire Returns of the Census of Religious Worship 1851* (1991), p.3.
11. W.T. Whitley (ed.), *Church Books of Ford or Cuddington and Amersham* (1912), p.209.
12. Bucks Record Office BAS/1260/38.
13. B. Godwin, *Memoirs of Richard Morris* (1819).
14. N. Pevsner and E. Williamson, *The Buildings of England: Buckinghamshire*, 2nd edition (1994).
15. G. Lipscomb, *History and Antiquities of the County of Buckingham*, vol.3 (1847), p.179.
16. Bucks Record Office DC9/1/81.

Chapter Eight
Schools, pp.83-88
1. E.R.C. Brinkworth, *Episcopal Visitation Book for the Archdeaconry of Buckingham 1662* (1947), p.1.
2. Reports of the Charity Commissioners: Bucks (1819-37), p.8.
3. Bucks Record Office DC/9/1/81.
4. Bucks Record Office DC/9/1/81.

Chapter Nine
Caring for the Poor, pp.88-95
1. J.H. Laverty (ed.), *Amersham Parish Chest*, p.61.
2. Bucks Record Office D/DR/12/8.
3. Bucks Record Office D/DR/12/12.
4. Reports of the Charity Commissioners: Bucks (1819-37), p.20.
5. Laverty (ed.), *Amersham Parish Chest*, p.43.
6. N. Salmon, *The History of Amersham General Hospital 1838-1988* (1988).
7. Reports of the Charity Commissioners: Bucks (1819-37), p.27.
8. W. Page (ed.), *Victoria History of the County of Buckingham*, vol.3 (1925), p.155.

Chapter Ten
The Railway and Amersham on the Hill, pp.96-117
1. J.K. Fowler, *Echoes of Old Country Life* (1892), p.154.
2. C. Foxell, *The Story of the Metropolitan and Great Central Joint Line* (2000).
3. I. White, *History of Little Chalfont* (1993), p.60.
4. Bucks Record Office DVD/1/114.
5. *Studio Yearbook of Decorative Art* (1907), p.28.
6. *Studio Yearbook of Decorative Art* (1910), p.49.
7. Records of Amersham Public Utility Society.
8. *Bucks Examiner*, 26 Feb. 1926.
9. *Bucks Examiner*, 4 Sep. 1936.
10. Amersham & District Community Association, *Woodside Farm, Amersham, Past, Present and Future* (1956).

Index

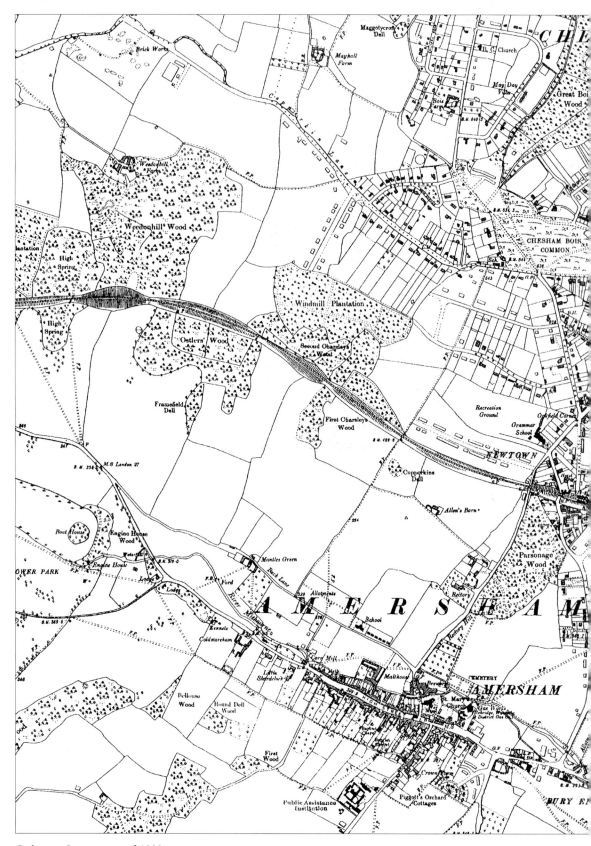

Ordnance Survey map of 1938